self-study workbooks

Handling Employees' Problems

Second Edition

Russell Tobin

KOGAN PAGE

© Copyright Russell M Tobin 1996, 2000

All rights reserved. No part of this publication may be reproduced, stored in a retrieval system, or transmitted in any form by any means, electronic, mechanical, photocopying, recording or otherwise without the prior permission of Kogan Page.

First published by Fenman in 1996
Second edition published by Kogan Page in 2000

Kogan Page Limited	Stylus Publishing Inc.
120 Pentonville Road	22883 Quicksilver Drive
London N1 9JN, UK	Sterling, VA 20166, USA

British Library Cataloguing in Publication Data.
A record for this book is available from the British Library.

ISBN 0 7494 3213 6

Printed and bound in Great Britain by Biddles Ltd, Guildford and King's Lynn

CONTENTS

	Page
Introduction	1
How this book can help you	1
How to use this book	2
What support is available?	3
What sort of problems does this cover?	5
How can complaints cause difficulty?	6 *
A framework of critical steps	9
Deciding whether to use these skills	10
Practical Leadership Skills	11
Demonstrations	13
Introduction	13
1. A cash-flow problem	14
2. Giving notice to leave	21
3. Delays on a building site	29
4. Fire danger in the office	35
5. Safety in a warehouse	41
6. Too much work	47
Comparisons with situations at your workplace	55 *
The critical steps explained further	59 *
A word on assertiveness	80 *
How you can go wrong	81
Coaching questions	85 *
Exceptional situations	111
'Yes, but...?' and 'What if...?'	111
Trying it out	119
One step at a time, then all together	119
Rehearsal exercise	125
Summary	129
Working towards a qualification?	130
A reminder card	131

* Your boss/coach/mentor may want to see these pages after completion.

Copyright © Russell M Tobin 2000, published by Kogan Page

INTRODUCTION

You may spend as much as eighty per cent of your time in work-centred discussions, and up to half of that time will go on handling problems, queries and complaints raised by your people. How you handle these discussions will significantly influence your personal productivity and thus your success as a manager or team leader.

HOW THIS BOOK CAN HELP YOU

This workbook can help you to reach practical solutions in these situations, in a way that helps you to develop your staff whilst avoiding unnecessary extra work for yourself. In turn that will reduce workload stress for you – and for your staff.

- It sets out five steps which are critical for success.

- It offers demonstrations of these critical steps being used with different types of people with a range of problems.

- It helps you to examine, and improve, your own work situation and work practices.

- And it answers some of your 'Yes, but...?' and 'What if...?' questions.

How this workbook relates to others in the series, especially the foundation book on Practical Leadership Skills, is illustrated below.

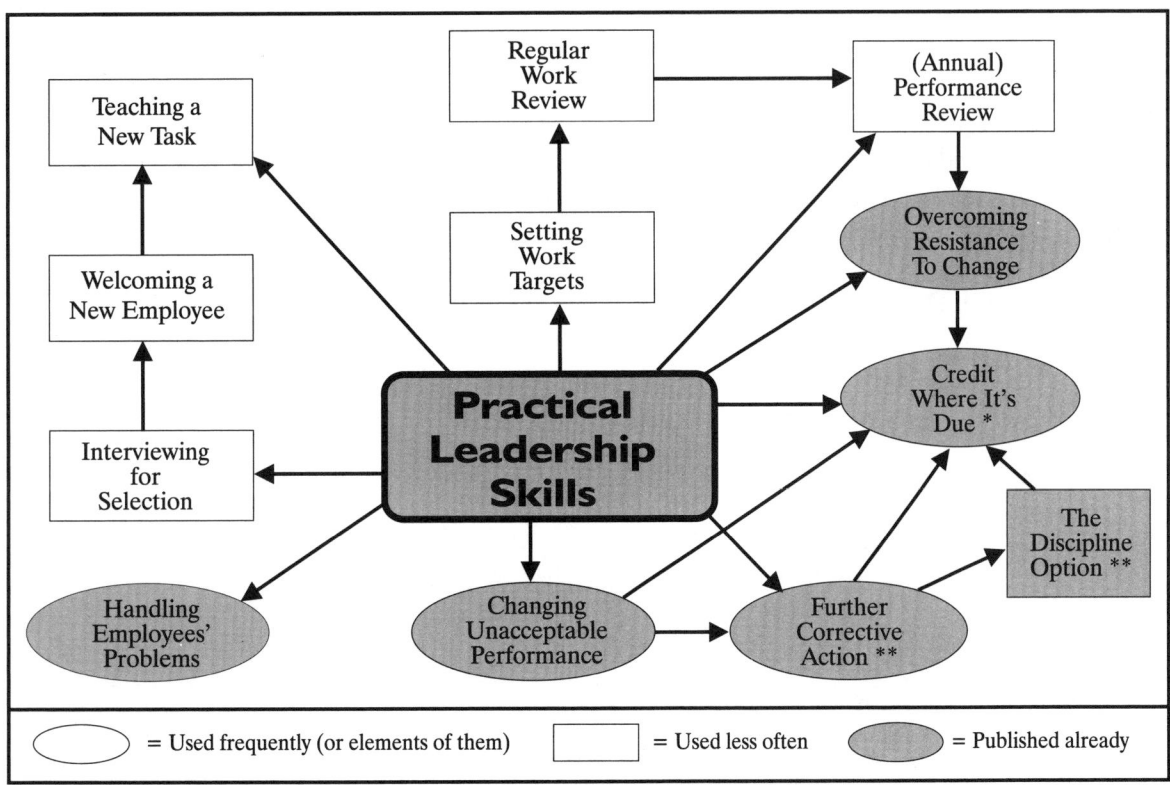

* First published as 'Recognising Dependable Work'.   ** These are combined in one book which will help to avoid claims against you.

Copyright © Russell M Tobin 2000, published by Kogan Page

HOW TO USE THIS BOOK

Work methods

You can read all this material and complete the exercises – which have a picture of a pen in the margin, as here – in two to three hours if you tackle it in one sitting. Or you can work through the sections in small chunks according to priorities that you set for yourself.

The exercises, and the author's comments on them, help you to examine ideas, and to look at your own work situation from a fresh viewpoint. If any of the questions make you feel uncertain then ask for help; some sources of help are shown on the next page.

You will see from the Table of Contents that the book is organised to help you dip into different areas of interest as you wish. So keep it available in your bookshelf for whenever you have a problem connected with handling employee problems and complaints.

There is a whole section on trying out the skills, so use every opportunity you can to put the tips into practice. Experiment, get feedback, persevere.

This book is best read after *Practical Leadership Skills* which is the foundation for the whole series of workbooks. If you haven't read it, but you need to deal quickly with an employee complaint or other problem, you should still try to read it later.

WHAT SUPPORT IS AVAILABLE?

If you are taking this module as one part of a development programme, or on your own initiative, there are several people who can help you.

YOUR BOSS — Who wants you to succeed. He or she may also be your COACH, especially with regard to the items marked in the Table of Contents with an asterisk (*). If your boss would like a quick refresher on coaching then 'A page for the boss' in the workbook *Practical Leadership Skills* provides just that.

> If you don't have a boss, see the second paragraph under AUTHOR below.

COLLEAGUES — Who want members of their team to be effective. They also know that if they give help to you they can request help from you later.

YOUR STAFF — Who also have a vested interest in your being effective. Because they see you as no one else sees you, you can ask them to give you objective feedback.

YOUR MENTOR — If you have a separate mentor or tutor, that person is there specifically to help you to succeed.

THE AUTHOR — Who offers further books, shown on page 1, which help with the all-the-time skills of practical leadership and the skills for specific and important discussions. All these books demonstrate the Practical Leadership Skills being applied in a range of situations.

He also runs short workshops where you can develop and check out your skills. Telephone 01280 817918.

If the first three know what you are doing – and you may need to tell them – they can help you. Why not enlist their support? Mutual support is good teamwork.

Why not list overleaf those people who could help you? In particular, check if anyone else is working through any of the workbooks in this series.

Copyright © Russell M Tobin 2000, published by Kogan Page

Notes

WHAT SORT OF PROBLEMS DOES THIS COVER?

People become concerned about all sorts of things: big work problems, little work problems, frustration with some situation or other, personal problems, real or imagined grievances about other people, and so on.

But only when they raise the problem or voice a complaint do you learn about these things, and people complain in all sorts of ways. When they do they want you to listen and they usually have some expectations of you. That can create a burden for you and, if you are not careful, you can make it heavier.

So a complaint is when someone voices a concern and you have to decide how to proceed with the discussion. You'll notice that we do *not* say, 'and you have to take action'. Whether or not to take some action is a decision that comes later in the discussion.

This simple definition covers many situations at work and the framework of skills offered here will help you to deal with them.

A complaint which appears trivial to a manager may be very serious to an employee. Insensitive handling can thus lead to problems growing out of all proportion.

So when someone comes to you with a worry, a grievance or a work problem it might not be the complaint itself which is important but the way in which it is handled.

NB   The first word in the title of this workbook is important. It is 'Handling', not 'Resolving'. Even when you handle problems superbly some people will still not get what they want. You can't please all the people all the time but you can handle them and their problems *effectively*.

Handling Employees' Problems

HOW CAN COMPLAINTS CAUSE DIFFICULTY?

Let's start with three hard questions and then go on to an easy one. Take a few minutes to ask these questions of your fellow managers or team leaders, and yourself.

1. 'When employees come to their boss with a problem of some kind, how can the boss *mishandle* the discussion?' Please note your answers below *before* you turn the page; your notes will be useful to you later on. There is one idea already to start you off.

> The boss listens badly or not at all.

2. If a boss should handle a problem *badly*, what are the likely immediate consequences?

3. If employees believe, rightly or wrongly, that their boss is bad at handling their problems, what are the likely long-term consequences of that belief?

Some answers are on page 7.

Some answers

1. The first question was, *'When employees come to their boss with a problem of some kind, how can the boss mishandle the discussion?'* Managers in workshops, speaking from experience, usually say things like:

   - The boss listens badly or not at all.
   - They don't give you time to explain properly.
   - They take it personally and get angry.
   - They try and brush it under the carpet.
   - They start to tell you all their problems when you just want yours sorted out.
   - They try to solve the problem before they fully understand it.
   - They pass the buck.
   - They blame you for the problem.
   - They promise to do something but don't.
   - They belittle the problem, they can't see how serious it is for you.
   - They become evasive and throw up a smokescreen.

Obviously, people make judgements about the way their problems are handled.

2. *The likely immediate consequences* are that the problem doesn't get solved and may well become worse. And the employee then has a further source of dissatisfaction.

3. *Likely long-term consequences* include a workforce that is less productive than it could be, problems are not raised because 'they (the bosses) don't want to know', the boss loses support from his people. Teamwork and output suffer.

   In an extreme case the employee will leave – either immediately or later; probably at maximum inconvenience to the manager.

Handling Employees' Problems

Here is a follow-up question

Have you ever known those immediate or long-term consequences to operate – to any extent? Can you say how they operate and why? (Think of when *you* have complained.)

Here is the easy question

'When employees come to their boss with a problem of some kind, what kind of behaviour are they hoping for – from the boss?'

If you would like a clue, think about how *you* have felt when you have gone to the boss with a problem that worried you. How do *you* want to be handled? Write down the steps the boss ought to cover – in sequence and in some detail. Then compare yourself with the experts.

Comments are on the next page.

Comments

You probably made a list of steps rather like those below which comprise:

A FRAMEWORK OF CRITICAL STEPS
for
HANDLING EMPLOYEES' PROBLEMS

1. **Listen attentively to the employee's complaint, ensure that you fully understand it, take notes.**

   Give total attention, clarify, check understanding, SUMMARIZE.

2. **Show that you understand his feelings and thank him for raising the matter.**

   Put yourself in his shoes. Show you want to know about problems.

3. **State your own position undefensively and without hostility.**

   Show where you stand. Don't cover up or attack back.

4. **Find out if the employee has any suggestions for resolving his complaint.**

   You may simply ask 'What do you think?' or coach the employee to think of options.

5. **If applicable, specify what you will do to correct the situation.**

   Only if applicable. It is usually better for people to solve their own problems.

You may have made some points which are not covered above. Or which contradict some of those above, or you may have a different sequence. Whichever, your points should be covered in the section entitled, 'The Critical Steps Explained Further'.

The five-step framework above, used with the (still to come) seven 'Practical Leadership Skills', will enable you to handle most employee problems and complaints that come to you.

> Where you read 'he' or 'his' will you please include 'or she'/'or hers'. This is to avoid clumsy language and no discrimination, prejudice or bias is intended.

Copyright © Russell M Tobin 2000, published by Kogan Page

DECIDING WHETHER TO USE THESE SKILLS

Whenever someone comes to you, in person or on the telephone, you use the first part of the first step – 'Listen attentively...' Or you ought to. For most people, however, this does not come automatically, they have to work at it.

In any case, if someone comes to you with a complaint you *have* to handle it one way or another; this framework helps you to do so effectively. As you listen you assess why the person has come to you, and you decide whether to work through the remainder of this framework step by step.

The chances are that you already use checklists (or models or guidelines) for other important parts of your job and a framework of critical steps is another one; you flesh it out in your own way and according to the employee and the situation.

Why 'critical' steps?

The sequence of the steps is important and the words in each have been carefully chosen. You don't have to follow the framework slavishly but, if you miss a step or go out of sequence, success may be harder. Be ready to re-enter the framework where you left off, or you may even need to return to the beginning.

If you follow these steps you will be more in control of yourself, and of the situation, as your actions influence the other person's reactions. And even if you do not reach a solution at once you will probably have done as well as possible. A well-structured discussion saves time and reduces misunderstandings, stress, and risk of failure.

As with all the frameworks for interpersonal skills in these workbooks the foundation framework of Practical Leadership Skills (PLS) is used in the background. You can see on the next page how the PLS framework relates to Handling Employees' Problems.

In the demonstrations later you can then see how both frameworks are used. Whilst this workbook focuses mainly on discussions with individual employees, the skills can also be used with your colleagues, with suppliers and (with one change) with customers.

PRACTICAL LEADERSHIP SKILLS

The framework of seven all-the-time Practical Leadership Skills is always in the background. Here it is as a reminder and you can see how the steps of Handling Employees' Problems (HEP) fits in with it.

1. **Maintain or enhance the self-esteem of the employee.**

   When you use HEP you enhance the self-esteem of the employee because you listen, empathise, share information and work towards a solution as a team.

2. **Don't attack the person, FOCUS ON THE PROBLEM.**

   You establish the facts of the problem and the feelings which led to it being raised. You can then sum up the whole problem now to be solved.

3. **Don't assume that the employee has committed an offence.**

   Some people are more ready to complain than others. Don't assume they do this out of malice or that, every time they approach, they want to complain.

4. **Encourage the employee to express his opinions and make suggestions.**

   You encourage opinions in HEP 1 and 2 and suggestions in HEP 4.

5. **Allow the employee adequate time to think through the problem and to suggest a solution.**

   Raising the problem in HEP 1 and 2 helps people to think it through. The pace of a well-structured discussion does the same thing.

6. **Ensure that the employee has an appropriate ACTION programme.**

   Sometimes the employee will have a solution, which you bring out in HEP 4, and he only needs your approval. Avoid doing the employee's work yourself.

7. **Always set a specific follow-up date.**

   This avoids problems being swept under the carpet or being left to fester. It also avoids false promises.

Copyright © Russell M Tobin 2000, published by Kogan Page

If you have not already worked through the book on Practical Leadership Skills, now could be a good time for you to do so.

Notes

DEMONSTRATIONS

INTRODUCTION

There are six examples of different bosses using the framework for Handling Employees' Problems (plus the Practical Leadership Skills framework) in their own different ways. They are applicable in a wide range of situations and industries.

1. A cash flow problem   14
   Helping with a personal problem, and taking less than four minutes.

2. Giving notice to leave   21
   In a busy steakhouse. Taking less than five minutes with both parties gaining.

3. Delays on a building site   29
   Where one trade impinges on another. Taking just two minutes to sort out the initial problem plus preventing a recurrence.

4. Fire danger in the office   35
   Requiring immediate action and with the manager at fault – less than four minutes.

5. Safety in a warehouse   41
   Requiring some self control from the boss, and taking about three minutes.

6. Too much work   47
   Holding firm and coaching four people through a serious problem in about six minutes.

   Comparisons with situations at your workplace.   55

With each demonstration you'll find comments on what the boss is doing as he or she follows the framework. At the end of each demonstration you will be asked to check the boss's performance against the PLS. And at the end of this section you will be asked how the demonstrations compare with situations in your own workplace, so please think about that as you read them.

After studying the demonstrations and later explanation of the steps, you may find yourself saying, 'Yes, but...?' or 'What if...?' and so on. Most of your questions should be answered in the section on Exceptional Situations.

1. A CASH-FLOW PROBLEM

Background

The boss in this situation is Brian. The employee is Keith, a Computer Technician who has recently transferred within his organisation from one part of the country to another.

After about seven months in his new job Keith asks if he can have a discussion with his boss about a personal matter and they meet in Brian's office.

NB   The comments on the right of the dialogue explain how the boss is using the critical steps. Please read the demonstration with a pencil in your hand to mark the text.

For a better understanding of the critical steps read the section, 'The Critical Steps Explained Further'.

	DIALOGUE	COMMENT
1.	Listen attentively to the employee's complaint, ensure that you fully understand it, take notes.	

Brian: 'Have a seat Keith and tell me, how can I help you?'

Bringing Keith quickly to the reason for the meeting.

Keith: 'Well, you know when I transferred down here...'

Brian: 'It's six months or so now, isn't it?'

Keith: 'Well, it's seven months now and we've had time to get settled in...'

Brian: 'Hm hm.'

Quietly encouraging Keith to talk.

Keith: 'And, er, we've been looking at how the budget's working out.'

Brian: 'The home budget, you mean?'

Brian checks if they are talking about work or not.

Keith: 'Yes...'

Brian: 'Go on.'

No need to think of a question.

Keith: 'And what we're finding is that, er, income is exceeding expenditure.'

Brian: 'I see, how serious is it?'

An open question. Brian can probe further if necessary.

Keith: 'Well, nobody told us how expensive this area is, and with the children costing us more and more, we're dipping into savings. I was wondering how I stand for a rise?'

Brian: 'On top of the increase when you moved here?'

This is a reminder to Keith, if one were needed.

Keith: 'Yes, I'm afraid so.'

Brian: 'What sort of amount do you have in mind?'

This is to establish the size of the problem.

Keith: 'Well, I was thinking of a sort of interim rise until the next pay review.'

Brian: 'An interim rise?'

Probing gently.

Keith: 'Yes, not a lot really, all we need is another

fifty a month but with tax and National Insurance I need to ask for a hundred.'

Brian: 'Okay, let me see if I've got you right. Now that you've settled in you're finding that your income, even after your rise, is not enough to cope with your expenses. Is that about right?'

Summarizes in order to check his understanding. Keith can correct him if he gets it wrong.

Keith: 'Yes, and the children are getting more and more expensive.'

| 2. | Show that you understand his feelings and thank him for raising the matter. |

Brian: 'Well, it's obviously going to be worrying for you, I can see. And I don't expect your wife is happy about money problems either.'

Shows that he also understands the other worries that go with money problems.

Keith: 'No, in fact it's been a bit of a strain, we thought we'd be a lot better off and it's come as a shock to find that we're not.'

Keith doesn't deny that.

Brian: 'Yes, I can imagine. Anyway, I'm glad you've raised the problem with me, Keith, because...'

This lets Brian move smoothly into Step 3.

| 3. | State your own position undefensively and without hostility. |

Brian: '... money problems can be really bad and I'd like to see yours sorted out.'

Brian is starting from the desire to see it sorted out; very positive and undefensive.

Keith: 'Well, I don't suppose I'm the first one to have a problem with personal cash flow.'

Brian: 'No, and you won't be the last, I'm sure. Keith, I want to help as far as I can but the bad news is that I can't do that by making an exception to the pay review policy. Personal money problems are not a reason to do that.'

The negative comes after the positive.

With a sound reason.

Keith: 'Oh, my goodness.'

Brian: 'But the good news is that, as you said yourself, you're not the first person to have a cash-flow problem.'

True enough. Keith is not alone.

Keith: 'Perhaps not, but I can't help feeling I'm the

most important one right now.'

| 4. | Find out if the employee has any suggestions for resolving his complaint. |

Brian: 'I agree Keith, so let's see what can be done. If I can't help by raising your income, and you're worried about exceeding it, what options do you have about your outgoings?'

Brian restates the whole problem and then focuses on the problem to be solved.

Keith: 'What do you mean?'

Brian: 'Well, you either need to reduce your spending or find additional income.'

He outlines the two stark options.

Keith: 'Well, Sophie can't go out to work, not with two young children.'

Brian: 'And you're in a full-time job yourself.'

Keith: 'I don't know how we can reduce spending, that's why I'm asking for a pay rise.'

Brian: 'Well, given the relocation package and the rise you did get, which was fairly substantial, what's happened to raise your spending Keith, can you think of anything new since you moved here?'

Brian focuses on what might have changed.

Keith: 'Yes, I can, several things, not to mention the bigger mortgage. That took up all the increase.'

Brian: 'Yes, I know, I've done that myself. Look, Keith, I don't want to get too close to your personal affairs so let me ask you; if you came to me with a budget for a new project and I said we couldn't afford it, what would you do?'

A coaching question to get Keith thinking on familiar lines.

Keith: 'I'd go away and rework it, I suppose.'

And it works.

Brian: 'Right, you'd go through it with a fine-tooth comb, see where you could make some savings, yes?'

Brian builds on the response.

Keith: 'True enough. Is that what you think I ought to do?'

Brian: 'Well, if you can't raise your income, what do you think?'

Brian wants Keith to come to that conclusion himself.

Handling Employees' Problems

Keith:	'Well, if I can't have a rise I suppose we'll have to. Perhaps we might have taken on too much when we moved into the new house.'	*And he does.*
Brian:	'Do you mean the house itself or all the things that go with it?'	*Narrowing down the options.*
Keith:	'It's some of the things we got on H.P. I think we both felt a bit flush. Got a bit carried away, I suppose.'	
Brian:	'So there might be some scope there. Are you saying that it would be a good idea to rework your budget, is that it?'	*Firming up on the sensible option, but by asking a question.*
Keith:	'Yes, that's what I'll have to do, I don't know how, but I'll have to have a go at it.'	*He can think about his budget on his own.*

> **5.** If applicable, specify what you will do to correct the situation.

Brian:	'Good, I expect you'll fix it one way or another. But, having said that, I know how worried I've been over money problems myself. The thing is, to be able to see your way through to a solution.'	*Avoiding involvement.* *It is good empathy to show that you have had this sort of problem yourself.*
Keith:	'Yes.'	
Brian:	'So I'm going to ask you to come and see me when you've worked things out. I shan't ask for the details but I do want to know that you're on top of it.'	*This problem has potentially serious consequences and Brian wants to see it dealt with.*
Keith:	'Okay.'	
Brian:	'Is tomorrow morning too soon? At nine o'clock? Just stick your head in and tell me how you got on.'	*The sooner it is handled the sooner Keith will be able to concentrate on his work.*
Keith:	'All right.'	
Brian:	'Let me get that in my diary then... "Keith" and a question mark.'	*Showing that he really wants it to happen.*
Keith:	'Okay, thanks Brian.'	
Brian:	'That's all right. I'd rather have it sorted out than possibly getting worse.'	*Still showing concern.*

That discussion took less than four minutes, about one per cent of a normal working day. Check it against the framework for

PRACTICAL LEADERSHIP SKILLS

Do you agree that the boss used all seven of these all-the-time skills?

1. **Maintain or enhance the self-esteem of the employee.**

   Brian did this in two ways: by showing he and others had been in the same situation, and by helping Keith to see a way through to a solution.

2. **Don't attack the person, FOCUS ON THE PROBLEM.**

   There was no attacking or hostility. The boss quickly focused on the choice for the employee to make between two basic options.

3. **Don't assume that the employee has committed an offence.**

   There was no assumption about foolish spending or anything like that.

4. **Encourage the employee to express his opinions and make suggestions.**

   Yes, first by good listening and empathy, and then with a question that helped the employee to relate his problem to his work experience.

5. **Allow the employee adequate time to think through the problem and to suggest a solution.**

   Less than four minutes in the discussion, and then overnight.

6. **Ensure that the employee has an appropriate ACTION programme.**

   He will rework his budget without delay.

7. **Always set a specific follow-up date.**

   Soon, in order to give urgency to the action plan. The boss might ask for a broad outline of the plan but will not want to go into the details.

Copyright © Russell M Tobin 2000, published by Kogan Page

Notes

2. GIVING NOTICE TO LEAVE

Background

In this situation the boss is Sarah, who manages a steakhouse which is part of a chain. She has just returned from a residential training course on staff management skills and is on duty for the evening session.

At the end of the session she is approached by Lisa. She is one of Sarah's part-time waitresses and a very good employee who has been with the company for several months. Sarah knows that Lisa works three evening sessions each week and that she is married with two grown-up children.

It is Thursday evening and Sarah is in her small office when Lisa comes along.

NB   The comments on the right of the dialogue explain how the boss is using the critical steps. Please read the demonstration with a pencil in your hand to mark the text.

For a better understanding of the critical steps read the section, 'The Critical Steps Explained Further'.

Handling Employees' Problems

DIALOGUE	COMMENT

> 1. Listen attentively to the employee's complaint, ensure that you fully understand it, take notes.

Lisa:	'Have you got a minute Sarah?'	
Sarah:	'Yes, of course Lisa, what is it?'	*Sarah starts listening attentively.*
Lisa:	'Well, I'm sorry Sarah, but I've got to give you my notice.'	*This is the ultimate complaint.*
Sarah:	'Oh dear, that's not something I want to hear, Lisa. What's the problem?'	*Immediately shows concern.*
Lisa:	'It's nothing to do with you Sarah, or the company, it's just that I need the extra money.'	
Sarah:	'Oh, I see. Does that mean you've got another job then?'	*Gently probing.*
Lisa:	'Well, we were in The Entwhistle last weekend and the manager, he's seen me working here, and we got chatting and, I don't know how it came up, really, but he finished up offering me the same sort of work, and the same sort of money but more sessions.'	*The Entwhistle is another pub that serves meals.*
Sarah:	'I see. Well, The Entwhistle's all right, I know. That's George somebody isn't it?'	*Sarah is careful not to criticize Lisa's choice as this would be to criticize her.*
Lisa:	'Yes, George Accrington. I get on all right with him, and the place seems all right.'	
Sarah:	'I think you'd get on all right with just about anybody, Lisa. So, are you moving just for the money, is that it?'	*A compliment, and a question to check her understanding.*
Lisa:	'Yes, that's all it is. I think Eric had just said how his firm had cut back on overtime, you know, and we got to talking about all the expenses people have. Then George asked me how many hours I did here.'	*Sarah knows that Eric is Lisa's husband.*
Sarah:	'Mmmm.'	*'Keep talking.'*
Lisa:	'I said "three evenings a week" and he said he was looking for somebody to do five.'	

Sarah:	'All in one go, eh?'	*Seeking information.*
Lisa:	'Well, I think someone must have given their notice in.'	
Sarah:	'Or do you think business is picking up at The Entwhistle?'	*Looking for more information **and** to get Lisa thinking how secure the new job will be.*
Lisa:	'Well, it didn't look any busier than usual, I didn't think so anyway.'	
Sarah:	'Hmm, so he offered you the job did he?'	*More checking.*
Lisa:	'Well, he asked me if I'd like to do it and I thought about the extra hours and the extra tips and I couldn't say no, not really.'	
Sarah:	'And it's nothing to do with working here?'	*Double checking.*
Lisa:	'Oh no, I've always enjoyed it here. It's just the extra money.'	
Sarah:	'Well, I'm glad that's the only reason. And when are you expecting to start there?'	*Or, in other words, 'How long do I have you here?'*
Lisa:	'Well, he said I could start as soon as I wanted but I said I'd work my notice here, do things properly.'	
Sarah:	'Okay. Does that mean you've definitely accepted the job Lisa?'	*Looking for firm facts.*
Lisa:	'Well, yes, I suppose so, that's how we left it anyway.'	

2.	Show that you understand his feelings and thank him for raising the matter.

Sarah:	'Lisa, I can see that you need to earn some extra money and I can certainly understand that you don't want to look a gift horse in the mouth. But it does sound as if you wouldn't be moving if you were getting enough money here. Would that be right?'	*Sarah puts herself in Lisa's shoes.* *Then she checks her own understanding of Lisa's total feelings.*
Lisa:	'Yes, I've never had any problems here. Everybody's been fine. But we're looking at a lot of money over a year.'	
Sarah:	'Yes. Anyway, thanks for talking it over with me because it does give me the chance to tell you where I stand on this.'	*Lisa was entitled to just hand in her notice and not discuss it.*

Handling Employees' Problems

3.	State your own position undefensively and without hostility.

Sarah: 'I think Lisa, that good people are worth keeping and you're good, so I don't want to lose you, not if I can help it.'

Two parts to her position, both clear, both positive and both undefensive.

Lisa: 'Hmm.'

Sarah: 'And if I had known that you needed to earn extra money I would have done what I could to help.'

A third part, equally clear.

Lisa: 'Well, I didn't really know myself. It's just that when Eric has his overtime cut, there's George Accrington showing us how to make it up. It's an offer I can't refuse. And Eric will do some of the housework when I'm out, or so he says.'

More information.

Sarah: 'Well, you've got that one covered.'

4.	Find out if the employee has any suggestions for resolving his complaint.

Sarah: 'Look Lisa, I'd like to find a way to keep you here. You know what we're like, you've been happy enough, and I don't want you to leave, so what can we work out?'

This follows from Sarah's position. She avoids leaping to Step 5 with an equal offer of extra hours. Instead she restates the problem, from both points of view.

Lisa: 'Well, I feel as if I'm blackmailing you now.'

Sarah: 'Yes, I know, it's a bit embarrassing, and that's why I'm not trying to offer you more than The Entwhistle. I just want to see if we can work something out that suits us both.'

More empathy from Sarah. Then more on her position and back to solving the joint problem.

Lisa: 'I'm not sure that we can really.'

She probably feels that Sarah won't offer her the same terms.

Sarah: 'Okay. You said that Eric had had his overtime cut; can I ask what that's worth in a week?'

Sarah focuses on the size of Lisa's problem.

Lisa: 'Not sure really, it's not all stopped but we can't rely on it any more.'

Sarah: 'So you want to try and cover for all of it, just in case?'

Lisa: 'That's right. It's not a lot, a couple of hours twice a week.'

Now Sarah can estimate the size of the problem.

Sarah:	'Right. So if you could cover that, without spending more time at work than you have to, you'd be okay?'	*Sarah puts in something else for Lisa to consider.*
Lisa:	'Yes, that's right.'	
Sarah:	'Could you cover it if you had just one extra session, instead of two, bearing in mind the tips you'd get?'	*As Lisa has made no suggestions, Sarah uses a question to test an idea forming in her own mind.*
Lisa:	'I suppose I could, yes.'	

5.	If applicable, specify what you will do to correct the situation.

Sarah:	'Okay then. I said I'd have done what I could if I'd known you needed the extra money and, as it is, I think business is developing well enough for me to offer you another evening session.'	*Offering 'another evening session' is quite specific.*
Lisa:	'Oh.'	
Sarah:	'Yes, I've been wondering when to do something and this has made my mind up. I reckon Friday is busy enough for another person to come in.'	
Lisa:	'Friday...'	
Sarah:	'Yes, would be good for tips, I should think. You don't have the hassle of changing jobs and getting to know new people, and you'll earn the money you need in one session, not two. How do you feel about that?'	*Sarah actively sells the benefits of following her suggestion. She doesn't knock the other employer as this might alienate Lisa. She stays positive.*
Lisa:	'Well, all we need to do is cover Eric's overtime, yes.'	
Sarah:	'Yes, you'll carry on here?'	*Sarah seeks clear confirmation.*
Lisa:	'Yes. I didn't want to leave anyway.'	
Sarah:	'Lovely. I think you're doing the right thing Lisa. You don't want to be working five nights if you can manage with four.'	*And she confirms to Lisa that Lisa has done the right thing.*
Lisa:	'No, I don't.'	
Sarah:	'Grand. Now, do you have to say anything to George Accrington?'	*She is thinking about an appropriate action programme.*

Copyright © Russell M Tobin 2000, published by Kogan Page

Lisa:	'I should do, he'll be expecting me the Monday after next.'
Sarah:	'Well, at least he won't be any worse off and he'll have a week to find someone else.'	*Making two more positive points that reinforce Lisa's decision.*
Lisa:	'Hmm.'
Sarah:	'You're not looking forward to speaking to him are you?'	*Sarah understands Lisa's feelings again.*
Lisa:	'Hmm.'
Sarah:	'Look, why not telephone him, from here. You can simply say that you've changed your mind. You don't have to give a reason and it's not as if you've accepted a written offer from him.'	*Making it easier for Lisa.*
Lisa:	'When do I do my first Friday here, Sarah?'
Sarah:	'Tomorrow if you like, or you can leave it to next week, it's up to you.'	*Sarah knows that the time and expense of finding a new waitress far outweigh the cost of one session's wages.*
Lisa:	'I think tomorrow's a bit quick.'
Sarah:	'Okay, then. Do you want to give George a ring? Give him time to find someone else?'	*Gently moving her to dispose of the remaining problem.*
Lisa:	'Yes okay. If I can use the phone, it's better than going in there.'
Sarah:	'Okay. And next time you're in we'll work things out for next Friday.'
Lisa:	'Yes, thanks very much.'
Sarah:	'Well, I'm really pleased we could work something out that suits us both. All's well that ends well, eh?'
Lisa:	'Yes. Thanks.'

You can see that the boss followed the framework for Handling Employees' Problems. On the next page see how she also followed the framework of Practical Leadership Skills.

That discussion took less than five minutes, about one per cent of a normal working day – and far less time than would be needed to recruit and train a new employee. Check it against the framework for

PRACTICAL LEADERSHIP SKILLS

Do you agree that the boss used all these skills?

1. **Maintain or enhance the self-esteem of the employee.**

   Sarah did this in several ways, through her comments, her empathy and her position in wanting to keep good people.

2. **Don't attack the person, FOCUS ON THE PROBLEM.**

   There was no hostility. Sarah grasped Lisa's problem of reduced family income, then gauged the size of it so as to be able to match the shortfall.

3. **Don't assume that the employee has committed an offence.**

   Sarah clearly did not assume that she was being pressured for extra pay. On the contrary, she appreciated Lisa's thoughts that she might think so.

4. **Encourage the employee to express his opinions and make suggestions.**

   Yes, Sarah encouraged opinions and suggestions and then got Lisa's opinion on her own suggestion.

5. **Allow the employee adequate time to think through the problem and to suggest a solution.**

   About five structured minutes, a pace which allowed Lisa not to feel pressured.

6. **Ensure that the employee has an appropriate ACTION programme.**

   She will (a) stay at the steakhouse and (b) ring George Accrington now.

7. **Always set a specific follow-up date.**

   Next time Lisa is in to work. Quite specific.

Copyright © Russell M Tobin 2000, published by Kogan Page

Notes

3. DELAYS ON A BUILDING SITE

Background

This occurs on a building site where the General Foreman of a housebuilding company is doing his early morning rounds to inspect the work of the various tradesmen.

The tradesmen are from sub-contracting firms and the various trades follow each other, eg the carpenters start their work in a house after the plasterers move out.

The General Foreman is Alan and the Carpenter Foreman is Denis who has two teams on the site.

At about 8.15 am Alan is approaching Plot 22 where he expects to find Denis's carpenter colleagues at work inside the house. He is surprised to find them still outside with all their gear – and with Denis. Denis comes up to Alan as he arrives.

NB The comments on the right of the dialogue explain how the boss is using the critical steps. Please read the demonstration with a pencil in your hand to mark the text.

For a better understanding of the critical steps read the section, 'The Critical Steps Explained Further'.

Copyright © Russell M Tobin 2000, published by Kogan Page

Handling Employees' Problems

DIALOGUE	COMMENT

> **1.** Listen attentively to the employee's complaint, ensure that you fully understand it, take notes.

Denis: 'I want a word with you.'

Alan: 'What about, Denis?'   *Alan does not respond badly to the apparent rudeness.*

Denis: 'Well I want to know why you make such a fuss about costs, but you can still pay us for standing around doing nothing.'

Alan: 'You're ahead of me Denis, what do you mean?'   *Complaints are seldom announced as such, Alan is coming to the point via a devious route.*

Denis: 'Well, we get here, expecting to walk straight in and get on with the job, and the plasterers are still in there.'

Alan: 'I thought they'd be out of the way by now.'   *This is Alan's information.*

Denis: 'Well they're not, and it's not the first time either. We're trying to get started, and they're still moving out. How can we make money with this going on?'

Alan: 'So what have they got to do then? Because I know they've finished plastering.'   *Alan had seen, at the end of the previous day, that they had finished that work.*

Denis: 'Well, they're using the place as a storeroom, and they've still to clean the floor.'

Alan: 'I see. Yes, I hadn't realised. When do you reckon you can get in then?'   *Alan sees his own mistake and checks on the size of the problem.*

Denis: 'Another hour, at least, we're not going in until it's properly cleaned out.'

Alan: 'Not until about quarter past nine then?'   *Alan makes a note. He takes Denis's statement at face value.*

Denis: 'Yeah, an hour.'

> **2.** Show that you understand his feelings and thank him for raising the matter.

Alan: 'Okay, I can see that you're going to be under pressure now.'   *Alan can see Denis is fed-up about losing time.*

Denis: 'Dead right, and the lads are moaning about bonus. They're not earning when they're standing around, you know that well enough.'	Denis responds well and shows another important concern.
Alan: 'Right, giving you a hard time are they?'	Alan recognizes this and shows he understands. Without that, Denis would probably continue to complain until he did get some understanding.
Denis: 'Well, what do you think?'	
Alan: 'Yes. Well look Denis, it's always best that you tell me about problems like this because...'	Alan assures Denis that he has done the right thing by complaining.

> **3.** State your own position undefensively and without hostility.

Alan: '... obviously, I don't want you being held up. And I don't want you having aggro from your lads either. I'm sorry you've got this lot.'	'because' after the thanks leads naturally into Alan stating the three parts of his position.
Denis: 'Well, what about this then?'	Many bosses would respond to this by leaping into action. Indeed, Alan could do just that but he knows that Step 4 can give him a solution and more information.

> **4.** Find out if the employee has any suggestions for resolving his complaint.

Alan: 'Well, they're packing up now, you said, so what we've got to do Denis is make sure we don't have this again. Any ideas on that yourself?'	Alan could have promised that he would 'speak to' the plasterers but, right now, he focuses on problem-prevention in future.
Denis: 'Well, they're telling you they've finished, and maybe they have finished, but they haven't cleared out, and *that's* the problem.'	
Alan: 'Okay, so we've got to be sure they've *really* finished.'	Checks his understanding.
Denis: 'Yes. They're not really finished until they've cleaned up and moved out. And you've got to *see* they've finished.'	'Finished' means ready for the next trade to start work.
Alan: 'All right. Can you work round it this time Denis?'	Alan wants an appropriate action programme for the problem now.

Copyright © Russell M Tobin 2000, published by Kogan Page

Denis:	'Well, I will, but I don't see why we should always be working round other people. Last time, eh?'	Denis responds well because he has been handled well. He can re-arrange work to ensure time is well used.

> 5. If applicable, specify what you will do to correct the situation.

Alan:	'Okay, thanks Denis. What I'll do then is, next time, I'll make sure the place is ready for you, one hundred per cent, *before* you get there.'	Alan avoids saying anything about rebuking the plasterers. He still has to hear their explanation.
Denis:	'Yeah, okay.'	
Alan:	'Right. I'll see them now, and then I'll see you next time I'm round, about twelve; see how you're getting on.'	When Denis talks to his lads they will want to know what happened with Alan. Denis will be able to repeat Alan's action plan about avoiding the problem in future, and also say that Alan will be speaking to the plasterers now.
Denis:	'Okay, see you.'	

You can see that the boss has followed the framework for Handling Employees' Problems in his own way. On the next page you can see how Alan followed the framework of Practical Leadership Skills at the same time.

When Alan talks to the plasterers he will probably use the framework for Changing Unacceptable Performance – from a workbook of that name in this series.

That discussion took just two minutes, less than one per cent of a normal working day, to solve a current problem and avoid a future one. Check it against the framework for

PRACTICAL LEADERSHIP SKILLS

Do you agree that the boss used all seven of these all-the-time skills?

1. **Maintain or enhance the self-esteem of the employee.**

   Mainly through the empathy in Step 2 but also, and importantly, through an action plan for the future that Denis can take back to his people.

2. **Don't attack the person, FOCUS ON THE PROBLEM.**

   Alan didn't attack. He did work to make sure the problem didn't occur again. And he ensured Denis would have something positive for his lads.

3. **Don't assume that the employee has committed an offence.**

   Alan did not try, or need, to argue with Denis on his estimate of time lost.

4. **Encourage the employee to express his opinions and make suggestions.**

   Alan listened well, despite the initial rudeness of Denis. Then, by moving deliberately through the framework, he got more information and ideas for fixing a problem that, hitherto, had not really been appreciated.

5. **Allow the employee adequate time to think through the problem and to suggest a solution.**

   Having realised the problem, Denis had enough time, because of the pace of the discussion, to think through to a simple solution.

6. **Ensure that the employee has an appropriate ACTION programme.**

   Denis will 'work round it this time'. Alan could have specifically asked him to, eg, do some measuring up in empty rooms, but he didn't need to.

7. **Always set a specific follow-up date.**

   About twelve o'clock today.

Copyright © Russell M Tobin 2000, published by Kogan Page

Notes

4. FIRE DANGER IN THE OFFICE

Background

This takes place in the offices of a large company in the financial services sector. The company is expanding rapidly and space is becoming very tight. New premises are being acquired but until they are ready for occupation everyone is expected to 'make do and mend' so far as working conditions are concerned in the present premises.

In one department a great deal of copying is done, together with printing on four printers which is generated by a number of computer terminals.

The manager of this department is Jackie who is under continual pressure because of the company's expansion. She is making a copy of a document on the big machine near the fire exit when Simon comes along with something to copy on the same machine. He is a long-standing employee who is very conscientious but who is also known as a bit of a moaner.

NB   The comments on the right of the dialogue explain how the boss is using the critical steps. Please read the demonstration with a pencil in your hand to mark the text.

For a better understanding of the critical steps read the section, 'The Critical Steps Explained Further'.

Handling Employees' Problems

DIALOGUE	COMMENT
1. Listen attentively to the employee's complaint, ensure that you fully understand it, take notes.	

Jackie: 'Hello, Simon, I won't be a minute.'

Simon: 'That's all right, it's always a pleasure to watch a fortune teller at work.'

Jackie: 'Fortune teller? If I were I'd be winning the lottery.'

Jackie is puzzled by Simon's remark but not yet ready to take it up.

Simon: 'Well, I'm getting the impression that you can see into the future.'

Jackie: 'Simon, are you trying to tell me something?'

Now trying to get to the point.

Simon: 'Jackie, if there's a fire in this place we won't be able to get out this way, so you must be pretty confident that we won't have one before we move. I just wish I could look into the future like you do.'

Jackie looks round and sees many boxes of paper stacked on the floor blocking the way to the fire exit.

Jackie: 'Well, I can see what you mean. How long has this lot been here?'

She seeks more information and gives herself time to think.

Simon: 'You must have seen it, surely.'

Jackie: 'I suppose I must have done but... how long has this been going on?'

Jackie may have seen it but hadn't really taken heed of what she was seeing.

Simon: 'There's always been a couple of boxes for the copying machine, no problem. But then there were letterheads for the computer printers, continuation sheets, then quotation forms and now this place is a fire trap.'

Jackie: 'Yes, there must be twenty or thirty boxes here. How did we come to have this much?'

She assesses what she can see and still can't understand how it became so bad.

Simon: 'Well, as I say, it was just a couple of boxes, then there were four, then there were six. And when they were getting stacked up near the door you've *got* to be saying we're fireproof.'

36 *Copyright © Russell M Tobin 2000, published by Kogan Page*

Demonstrations

2.	Show that you understand his feelings and thank him for raising the matter.

Jackie: 'Hmm, were you thinking I didn't care?'

Simon: 'Well, I did wonder a bit.'

Jackie: 'Hmm, I'm not surprised you were worried. The way that lot's been dropped it's a potential death trap if we do have a fire.'

Simon: 'So what are you going to do about it then?'

Jackie: 'I'm going to make sure it's fixed, that's what. And I must say, I'm glad you've told me. If we did have a fire it doesn't bear thinking about.'

Simon: 'That's what I thought.'

3.	State your own position undefensively and without hostility.

Jackie: 'There's no two ways about it, we've got to have this exit clear. And we need it done now because you're right, we can't predict when a fire will come.'

Simon: 'Right.'

Jackie: 'But we still have to operate.'

4.	Find out if the employee has any suggestions for resolving his complaint.

Jackie: 'You've obviously been thinking about it Simon. What's the best way to keep operating but without taking a risk about fire?'

Simon: 'Well, I think we can stack three high against the wall but really there's only room on the floor for four boxes.'

Jackie: 'That's handy. We've got just the four

Jackie accepts that Simon's sarcasm was his way of raising the problem without showing alarm.

Good empathy.

An invitation to jump to Step 5 – Jackie has to be careful.

She starts to move into Step 3 but finishes Step 2 first. This helps her to avoid being defensive or hostile in the next step.

Indicating urgency and acknowledging that a fire can happen any time.

Concern for people is balanced with concern for the job.

They are still where the problem is and Jackie wants action started before leaving.

He has been thinking about it. Even if he hadn't he would still want to show that he has ideas.

Agreeing where she can.

Copyright © Russell M Tobin 2000, published by Kogan Page

	different products haven't we?'
Simon:	'For the moment we have, yes. But twelve boxes is the limit, I think. If we try to go higher than three boxes they'll be unstable.'
Jackie:	'And we'd be back to square one?'
Simon:	'That's right. So the rest have got to go.'
Jackie:	'I agree. The question, though, is where?'	*Jackie agrees. But she has no idea about where the excess can go.*
Simon:	'I've got an idea there as well.'	
Jackie:	'Go on, then.'	*She really wants Simon to come up with ideas.*
Simon:	'Well, looking at what we've got here, it looks like we're ordering eight boxes at a time.'	
Jackie:	'Yes, or we're calling it off like that from the supplier. It's Charlie who looks after that.'	*Agreeing, anticipating, and wanting to move the idea along.*
Simon:	'So, all we do then is call them off so that we never have more than three boxes. And we can ask the supplier to take the extras back right now. They can stay on their premises as well as ours. And they can deliver quickly enough if we get short.'	
Jackie:	'That's right, they're only round the corner. I think that's a lovely idea... Okay... I'll get Charlie on to that... but I really want to see this moving now, before I leave.'	*Jackie wants Simon to see how pleased she is with his thinking. She also reminds herself of the situation's urgency and sticks with Step 4.*
Simon:	'All right... Look, I'll sort three of each and I'll make sure we can get through to the door. Can you get Charlie to bring a barrow?'	*If Simon had not suggested this then Jackie would. But he has responded well.*
Jackie:	'I certainly can.'	*And so does Jackie.*

5.	If applicable, specify what you will do to correct the situation.

Jackie:	'Smashing. I'll get Charlie along right away. Will you tell him what you've done?'	*Confirming her previous response.*
Simon:	'Yes, okay, I'll show him what's to go.'	
Jackie:	'Right. I'll put him in the picture and he'll	*Indicating she will not place Simon*

have to speak to the suppliers. If I can rely on you to make it safe Simon, you can leave Charlie to take the excess to reception, okay?'	*in an awkward position with Charlie.* *And also that she is asking Simon to do only so much of the work.*
Simon: 'Fair enough.'	
Jackie: 'Okay. He should be along inside ten minutes. Will you come and let me know when you've handed over to him?'	*In this situation she wants to get an assurance that action is being taken.*
Simon: 'Will do.'	
Jackie: 'Okay. And thanks again Simon. There's no doubt we're better safe than sorry.'	*A very positive ending.*

Although the boss still has to speak with Charlie, you can see that with Simon she has followed very well the framework for Handling Employees' Problems – in her own way.

On the next page you can see how Jackie followed the framework of Practical Leadership Skills at the same time.

Handling Employees' Problems

That discussion took less than four minutes to settle a really important problem. Check it against the framework for

PRACTICAL LEADERSHIP SKILLS

Do you agree that the boss used all seven of these all-the-time skills?

1. **Maintain or enhance the self-esteem of the employee.**

   There was clear agreement with Simon's view of the safety problem and, after his ideas for a solution, Jackie thanked him again for raising it.

2. **Don't attack the person, FOCUS ON THE PROBLEM.**

   The risk in the case of a fire was one problem. The second was how Jackie's lack of prevention might have been badly perceived by staff.

3. **Don't assume that the employee has committed an offence.**

   Although Simon may be regarded as being something of a moaner, Jackie was careful to take his complaint on merit.

4. **Encourage the employee to express his opinions and make suggestions.**

   Jackie listened well in the beginning and then was happy to encourage suggestions from Simon. She had no ideas herself.

5. **Allow the employee adequate time to think through the problem and to suggest a solution.**

   Jackie guessed Simon would have thought about it already; she was right.

6. **Ensure that the employee has an appropriate ACTION programme.**

   There is action for Simon in sorting out the boxes and making safe. Then for Charlie to move the excess and avoid the problem in future.

7. **Always set a specific follow-up date.**

   Jackie expects to have Simon reporting back within about 15 minutes. She will expect Charlie to report back after talking with the supplier.

5. SAFETY IN A WAREHOUSE

Background

The boss in this situation is the manager in a large brewery warehouse containing a range of palletized products together with empty containers. The warehouse is served by several fork-lift trucks of two tons capacity and there are a number of employees employed on a racking line and on other duties.

This warehouse has many lines of storage racks.

The manager's office is in a corner of the building and the manager, Harry, is attending to paperwork in his office when one of the racking line employees barges in without knocking, and slams the door shut.

Harry is not accustomed to this sort of behaviour but chooses to handle the employee, Len, as effectively as he can. He knows Len to be a reasonable worker.

NB   The comments on the right of the dialogue explain how the boss is using the critical steps. Please read the demonstration with a pencil in your hand to mark the text.

For a better understanding of the critical steps read the section, 'The Critical Steps Explained Further'.

Handling Employees' Problems

DIALOGUE	COMMENT

> 1. Listen attentively to the employee's complaint, ensure that you fully understand it, take notes.

Len:	'Do we have to wait for somebody to get killed in this place? You can't walk around without some silly sod trying to run you down. I'm fed up with it.'	*It is not always that complaints are announced in such a forthright way.*
Harry:	'All right, I can see you're upset. Sit down and tell me about it.'	*Harry avoids saying, 'Calm down' because Len is entitled to be angry and would respond badly to that.*
Len:	'I was damn near killed. I'm walking past this aisle and out comes this fork-lift, couldn't have missed me by more than an inch. And I'll tell you something, this isn't the first time it's happened.'	*He does not become angry himself.*
Harry:	'Not the first time?'	*Harry prompts him to keep talking and does not have to think of questions himself.*
Len:	'No it isn't. Someone's going to get killed out there. They think all they've got to do is sound the horn and they don't have to look, not when they're coming out of an aisle anyway.'	
Harry:	'When was this Len?'	*A closed question for hard facts.*
Len:	'Just now. Look, I'm still shaking.'	*Len holds out his hands.*
Harry:	'Right. But you're not hurt then?'	*Harry looks and agrees. Asks the really important question.*
Len:	'Not this time, but I tell you, it was close.'	
Harry:	'Okay. Who was driving?'	*Looking for more facts.*
Len:	'Come on Harry, I'm not telling you that. But they're all the same out there. None of them are any good. They ought to be fired, the lot of them.'	
Harry:	'Well, what was he carrying then?'	*Harry does not get drawn into an argument about firing people.*
Len:	'Just returns, that's all. A pallet of returns.'	
Harry:	'Did he see you at all Len?'	
Len:	'I don't think so. He just reversed out and	

	shot away. He was gone.'	
Harry:	'Reversing, eh? Right. So where did this happen Len?'	
Len:	'It was the aisle between G and H. They seem to forget what they're driving, these guys.'	*Harry thinks he won't get more information at this time and decides to move to Step 2.*

> 2. Show that you understand his feelings and thank him for raising the matter.

Harry:	'Well, you must have been frightened to death Len, you were nearly run over, eh?'	*He has seen Len's hands shaking and heard him say he was 'damn near killed'.*
Len:	'You're not joking. Yes, I was frightened. And I'm *still* shaking.'	
Harry:	'Yes. So you're dead worried about your safety Len?'	*Harry sums it up in two words – 'your safety'.*
Len:	'Course I am.'	
Harry:	'Right. Well, thanks for coming to me Len. I'm glad you did because...'	*Len might have gone to the safety representative – and may do so still. Harry is ready to move forward.*

> 3. State your own position undefensively and without hostility.

Harry:	'... as far as I'm concerned, Len, you're entitled to walk around this place in safety. There's no doubt about that and it's my job to make sure you can.'	*Accepting responsibility – why try to evade it? – calms Len and helps him to switch to being positive.*
Len:	'Well, I couldn't agree more.'	*And it takes the wind out of Len's sails.*

> 4. Find out if the employee has any suggestions for resolving his complaint.

Harry:	'Right then. And it's not the first time, you said. Any ideas for solving the problem Len?'	*Harry uses what he has heard.*
Len:	'Well I think you ought to go out there and have a go at the lot of them. They're just a	

Handling Employees' Problems

	bunch of cowboys, they don't seem to care.'	
Harry:	'Hm. Perhaps I could talk to all the fork-lift drivers but I can't talk to anyone in particular, can I Len?'	Harry thinks this one over without committing himself. Says what he can not do.
Len:	'Well I think you should talk to all of them, they're all as bad as each other.'	
Harry:	'Well, that's one thing. And what about yourself Len, keeping yourself out of harm's way?'	Harry wants Len to focus on his own self-protection and to raise ideas for that.
Len:	'What do you mean, when I'm walking through the stores?'	
Harry:	'Yes, watching yourself at blind spots, at the end of aisles.'	Harry focuses on the problem as he understands it.
Len:	'Yes, right. Well, once is enough. Yes, I'll keep to the middle of the main aisle in future.'	And Len says the right words.
Harry:	'Okay. Do you want to tell me now who was driving?'	Another try at getting information.
Len:	'No, but you ask anybody out there. They're all the same.'	
Harry:	'Okay. Anything else, Len?'	A check before moving into Step 5.
Len:	'No. But I was lucky this time, haven't been injured. But it'll happen again to somebody, and they won't be so lucky, I can tell you.'	Much calmer now that he has been listened to.
Harry:	'Well, I want it safe, Len, so I'll tell you what I'll do.'	Restating his position.

5.	If applicable, specify what you will do to correct the situation.

Harry:	'I'll speak to the fork-lift drivers, but I can only do that in general terms, and I'll remind them all about safe practices, their training. And I'll emphasize this business of reversing out of blind aisles...'	Harry has now had time to firm up his thinking about what it is sensible for him to do.
Len:	'Right.'	Len waits for the next bit.

Harry: 'So that's what I'll do. Now, yourself, Len?'	*Checking that Len has taken on board his 'appropriate action programme'.*
Len: 'Don't you worry. I'll make sure I keep to the main aisle, and stay well away from blind corners.'	
Harry: 'Okay then. Right. Let's give it a week... from today Len. And I'll come to ask if you've seen any improvement in the warehouse. Okay?'	*Harry makes a note in his diary: 'Len – fork-lift safety.'*
Len: 'Okay.'	
Harry: 'Right, okay, thanks very much Len.'	
Len: 'Thank you.'	

On the next page you can check this discussion against the framework for Practical Leadership Skills.

Handling Employees' Problems

Harry kept that discussion on track by following the framework for Handling Employees' Problems. In about three minutes he defused and handled a potentially serious problem. Check how it went against the framework for

PRACTICAL LEADERSHIP SKILLS

Do you agree that the boss used all seven of these all-the-time skills?

1. **Maintain or enhance the self-esteem of the employee.**

   The key here is how Harry put himself into Len's shoes, showing it was understandable, and okay, to be 'frightened to death'.

2. **Don't attack the person, FOCUS ON THE PROBLEM.**

   Harry did not attack back after Len barged into his office. He then focused on ensuring that Len could be safe, through his own precautions as well as the driving practices of other staff.

3. **Don't assume that the employee has committed an offence.**

   Len has responsibility for his own safety but Harry did not assume he had been careless. That would have sparked off a row.

4. **Encourage the employee to express his opinions and make suggestions.**

   Harry first asked open questions and then closed questions for information. Then he got Len to focus on how he could keep himself safe.

5. **Allow the employee adequate time to think through the problem and to suggest a solution.**

   The time was adequate, given how Harry coached Len towards a solution.

6. **Ensure that the employee has an appropriate ACTION programme.**

   Len has his own plan for keeping out of harm's way.

7. **Always set a specific follow-up date.**

   A 'week from today' allows the boss to observe drivers in action, to reinforce safe practices and to deal with unsafe ones.

6. TOO MUCH WORK

Background

The boss in this situation is David, the Factory Manager on a large site of a multi-national company.

Over some years the number of staff, at all levels and in all functions, had become far higher than was really needed. The site had then become unprofitable and was in danger of being sold.

Recently, under new top management, one complete layer of management has been made redundant and Superintendents now supervise Foremen directly. There used to be several General Foremen coming between them.

Because of the urgent need to cut operating costs, the six General Foremen, plus two Superintendents, left at once with pay in lieu of notice. Their work was taken over by the four remaining Superintendents.

Some of the work of the General Foremen was on industrial relations issues and whilst the new urgency in the firm has reduced the power of the union representatives they have not gone away. In addition to losing their General Foremen, the Superintendents are also being asked to raise productivity.

All in all, the Superintendents – Terry, John, Mike and Erica – are under unaccustomed pressure and all four of them have been discussing their predicament. Terry has asked the Plant Manager to meet them and they are now sitting in David's office.

NB   The comments on the right of the dialogue explain how the boss is using the critical steps. Please read the demonstration with a pencil in your hand to mark the text.

For a better understanding of the critical steps read the section, 'The Critical Steps Explained Further'.

Handling Employees' Problems

DIALOGUE	COMMENT

> 1. Listen attentively to the employee's complaint, ensure that you fully understand it, take notes.

David: 'Okay, Terry, you mentioned a problem, something that you all wanted to raise?'	*Straight to the point.*
Terry: 'That's right. We've just been comparing notes, you know, and we all seem to be having the same sort of problems so we thought we ought to raise it without waiting for a regular meeting.'	*No interruptions from the boss.*
David: 'That sounds all right to me; what's the problem?'	
Terry: 'Well we feel like we're being stretched on the rack. The General Foremen did a lot of work and now we're having to do it all. And we know we've cut out a lot of communication problems but we haven't cut out the communication time; we still have to talk direct to the supervisors and the employee representatives.'	
David: 'Yes, I understand.'	*No comment yet but encourages Terry to keep talking.*
Terry: 'And we know that you said we had to cut out as much as we can, and we have done, but we've still got too much to do. We feel like we're on a treadmill, it never stops.'	
David: 'You're saying there's more pressure than there used to be?'	*David checks his understanding of the problem by reflecting what they say – but without agreeing.*
Terry: 'Not half. One way and another there's none of us leaving on time these days and we're all coming in early. The thing is, how long are we expected to go on like this? You know, if the guys on the shop floor... well, they wouldn't put up with it.'	
David: 'Go on.'	*Avoids being sidetracked and seeks to get the whole problem.*
Terry: 'Well, we're snowed under already and now you're wanting us to get higher efficiencies and reduced costs. We think you're asking too much David, that's what it is.'	

48 *Copyright © Russell M Tobin 2000, published by Kogan Page*

David:	'Right, let me see if I understand you properly. You're saying that since the reorganization you're all putting more time in. And, yes, I've seen that. And you're fully stretched with the work of the General Foremen without taking on the new initiatives as well. Have I got you right?'	A deliberate summarizing to check understanding and to help all of them. Pauses for a response.
Terry:	'Yes, we're *always* going to have their work. How can we be expected to take on more? We know we had a pay rise but there's only so much we can do.'	
David:	'And you're also saying that you've cut out as much work from the GFs as you can?'	Repeating an important point.
Terry:	'Yes, we have, but there wasn't much we could cut out, most of it was essential.'	And getting more information.
David:	'So you're working over, you can't reduce your workload and you can't handle anything new.'	With the background knowledge he already has David is now ready to move to Step 2.
Terry:	'That's about it David. We're not saying these things shouldn't be done. It's just that we can't see our way to doing them.'	

> 2. Show that you understand his feelings and thank him for raising the matter.

David:	'Okay. Well, you're obviously worried enough to bring it up with me. Are you wondering what might happen if we don't fix this lot?'	David is not sure about a second possible concern, regarding their jobs, so he asks.
John:	'Well, I can't say it hasn't crossed our minds. I mean, we think we're doing everything we can but, yes, we are worried. And we'd like some help, but we don't know what to ask for.'	And gets confirmation.
David:	'Right. I'm glad you've all spoken up because...'	Raising the problem took a lot of courage. David shows them that they were correct to do so.

> 3. State your own position undefensively and without hostility.

David:	'... I don't want you to fail, just as much as you don't want to fail.'	Very supportive.

Copyright © Russell M Tobin 2000, published by Kogan Page

Handling Employees' Problems

Terry:	'Yes.'
David:	'And you four were kept on because I thought that you, of all the Superintendents, were the guys to make it work.'	*Enhancing self-esteem, which must be pretty low.*
Mike:	'Well, we're having problems.'
David:	'Look, it's often the case that when you take on new responsibility you have to work extra hard to get on top of it.'	*A bit of education that needs to be stated as part of his position.*
Erica:	'That's what we're trying to do, and we're still snowed under.'
David:	'Yes, I understand that. And I also think that, with no more people, it could get harder before it gets better. But I do want it to get better.'	*Quite open with the bad news. But adding more support.*

---

4. Find out if the employee has any suggestions for resolving his complaint.

David:	'So if you have too much to do, how can you reduce your workload, that's the question.'	*Focusing them on the real problem to be solved.*
Terry:	'Well, we're not suggesting that we go back to having General Foremen but if we could have another Superintendent we could re-organise the work between us. And we'd still be down on headcount from before.'	*Putting forward the idea they first thought of, even though it goes against David's position of 'no more people'. They hope to persuade him.*
David:	'That's true enough. But let me remind you what we said at the time. We're so uncompetitive that we can't risk more expense. And the other thing is that we looked very carefully at how we should re-organise and four Superintendents was best. And it still is.'	*So David repeats his position. He goes back to the original reason for the redundancies with more of Step 3 (this happens often). He sees no reason to move from the original thinking.*
Terry:	'But we're doing the work of five, David.'
David:	'Terry, I don't dispute the hours you're putting in. I've seen you here when I arrive and often enough when I leave.'	*David knows the difference between activity (the hours they put in) and achievement (the output from those hours).*
Erica:	'I still think we need another person.'
David:	'Tell me what you've done so far.'	*This will help David assess what coaching he needs to do.*

Terry:	'Well, we've saved a fair bit of time on collating information.'	
David:	'From the supervisors?'	
Terry:	'Yes, and on the meetings we had with the GFs.'	
David:	'That's another couple of hours or more.'	
Terry:	'And we've shortened meetings with the supervisors.'	
David:	'Okay, anything else?'	
Terry:	'I think that's about it.'	
David:	'Okay. Look, you've all done the Time Management course? And that's strong on getting rid of time stealers? What can you apply from that?'	*David thinks this leaves plenty of scope for improvement and he moves forward by recalling relevant training.*
Terry:	'I don't know. I remember we did quite a few things after the course.'	*And gets some response.*
Mike:	'Yes, we delegated a fair bit of stuff to the GFs.'	
David:	'That's right, as I recall you planned to save about forty hours a week between the six of you, and that was just on delegation.'	*A reminder of what can be done (it was a good Time Management workshop).*
John:	'Yes, but the General Foremen have gone.'	
David:	'But you have supervisors, who also need to develop, and there were other tips in that course weren't there?'	*Prompting them to think of two areas.*
Mike:	'What do you mean?'	
David:	'Mike, I think we have the tools we need to reduce the workload but it's easy to forget about them. I know I'm using what I learned on that course because I've got just the same problem as you. I know you're here early because I'm here early.'	*What works for him should work for them.*
Erica:	'Okay. You're saying that we should go back to the course notes?'	*She takes the point from David's coaching.*
David:	'That sounds like a good idea, Erica. Do you remember the tip about backsliding?'	*Another coaching question.*

Handling Employees' Problems

Erica:	'No, was there one?'	
Terry:	'Yes, keeping a time log, wasn't it?'	*Often someone else in a group will have the answer.*
David:	'That's right, every six months, because we can *expect* backsliding. It's human nature.'	
Mike:	'So are you saying we should keep time logs?'	
David:	'Mike, what I'm hearing is that you, all of you, don't have time to do all that you need to do. So what do you think?'	*David reminds them that it is they who have the problem. And he puts the question back to them.*
Terry:	'Right, it's a start, isn't it?'	*They see that David is putting this ball back in their court. And they have to find some way of improving their situation if David will not change his position.*
John:	'We should see what we can do ourselves before we come to you, is that it?'	

> 5. If applicable, specify what you will do to correct the situation.

David:	'That's right, John, and what I'm going to do is set up a working party to look into this situation, and it's you four.'	*And David confirms that by pulling it all together.*
Mike:	'Thanks very much.'	
David:	'And I'll expect you to report back on the actions you're taking to reduce your workload. How long do you reckon you'll need?'	*This will get them to do some quick planning.*
Terry:	'Well, we'd better go through the course notes.'	*Teamwork comes into play.*
David:	'And if you do that you'll see all the gains that you made last time.'	*David voices his support very positively.*
John:	'Yes, and we'll need to keep time logs. For a week, do you think?'	*Tentative, looking for support from his colleagues.*
Mike:	'May as well, see what we're doing. But do we have the time?'	*Which he gets, but with a qualification.*
David:	'Well, without information it's hard to control anything. The analysis has to help.'	*David reinforces the team's direction.*
Erica:	'And then we'd better pool our ideas, what do you think?'	*Another tentative suggestion.*

Terry: 'Right, and then we'll know what we need to do, or we'll have a better idea anyway.'	*Which is taken up by another team member.*
David: 'So when do you want to report back?'	*Asking them to set a time limit.*
Terry: 'How about the regular production meeting, not next Friday, but the one after?'	*This gives them time to pool ideas and to make progress.*
David: 'Okay, that's the sixteenth. I'll put management productivity on the agenda. Right, is there anything else folks?'	*David is happy and looks to the others for any disagreement.*
Mike: 'We'll just have to wait and see.'	*Still somewhat dubious.*
David: 'Well, let me tell you. I've already done what you're going to do and I've cut out a load of stuff, one way and another. You saved yourselves a lot of time right after that course and I'm quite sure you'll be able to do it again.'	*More support and reassurance.*
Terry: 'Back to it then. Thanks David.'	

That focused discussion, taking only about six minutes, becomes the foundation for progress, and the work to achieve that progress will be done by the Superintendents. On the next page you can check how they managed against the framework of Practical Leadership Skills.

Copyright © Russell M Tobin 2000, published by Kogan Page

How did David do against the framework for

PRACTICAL LEADERSHIP SKILLS?

Do you agree that he used all seven of these all-the-time skills?

1. **Maintain or enhance the self-esteem of the employee.**

   David listened well. He pointed out they were the best people and then put them on their mettle to solve the problem. He finished with reassurance.

2. **Don't attack the person, FOCUS ON THE PROBLEM.**

   David focused on a problem with time management – where many helpful techniques were available from their course notes.

3. **Don't assume that the employee has committed an offence.**

   David avoided the worst assumption – that they would be unable to deal with the problem – although he had to coach them to an action programme.

4. **Encourage the employee to express his opinions and make suggestions.**

   David listened well and empathised. Then, with a firm platform of 'no more people', he asked how they could reduce their workload, and then how they could apply the time management techniques they had learned.

5. **Allow the employee adequate time to think through the problem and to suggest a solution.**

   They needed time to drop the idea of an extra person and think through techniques for improving time management. And they now have that time.

6. **Ensure that the employee has an appropriate ACTION programme.**

   This is to come up with their own action plan. They agreed their immediate action there and then.

7. **Always set a specific follow-up date.**

   David asked for it, they set it and, by the time they report back, they will have several actions underway.

COMPARISONS WITH SITUATIONS AT YOUR WORKPLACE

Most of these demonstrations will be from outside your own industry. To help you to make comparisons with your own situation, will you please examine other ways of looking at the demonstrations which are summarized below, and then write in your own examples.

1. A cash-flow problem

In this personal problem the boss could possibly feel some unnecessary guilt ('Nobody told us how expensive this area is'). The boss could also help the employee – if the boss were very kind and had the resources. It is also a situation where giving material help to one person could set an unfortunate precedent.

This demonstration shows well how the problem you define is the problem you solve. In Step 4, the boss brought together his own position and the employee's situation to focus on the type of solution required.

> What sort of situations are brought to you where it might be useful to redefine the problem, as was done in this demonstration?

Copyright © Russell M Tobin 2000, published by Kogan Page

2. Giving notice to leave

In this demonstration the boss was able to show the employee that she was on her side by the way she listened in Step 1, empathised with her in Step 2, and was then able to be very supportive in Step 3. As a result it became clear that the employee would be happy to stay if an arrangement could be made.

> Do you have any unsatisfactory situations where a (further) discussion using this framework, and being supportive, might be a good idea?

3. Delays on a building site

This is a classic example of one part of a team causing problems for another and where the immediate problem is quickly solved. But here the boss worked on avoiding a recurrence in the future. There are many situations where, having solved the immediate problem, it is sensible to look to the future as well.

> Are there any situations where the immediate problem has fallen away but you should be seeking to prevent it happening again?

4. Fire danger

Here the boss acknowledged, undefensively and without hostility, that she had failed to notice a high risk situation. Then, having asked herself, 'Why take the risk?' she went for immediate action using the employee's ideas.

> Have you had any situations where you felt that you may somehow have been at fault? And where, as a result, you might have denied the problem to some extent? If so, what situations should you now be reviewing?

5. Safety in a warehouse

Here the boss could have taken upon himself the whole task of finding a solution but was careful to seek ideas about what the employee could do for himself.

> Do you have any less-than-satisfactory situations right now where you should try seeking more ideas from the employees concerned?

Copyright © Russell M Tobin 2000, published by Kogan Page

6. Too much work

This shows a boss working with a group of people who, having forgotten effective techniques that they had previously learned, were hoping that the boss would get them out of an awkward situation. Instead the boss forced them to do the thinking they should already have done – and he left the problem with them.

> List typical situations where people ask for your help, and you give it – at some personal cost, in time and pressure.
>
> List them, then mark those where the employees could devise and implement solutions themselves if you looked to them, *and coached them*, to do so.
>
> This can be a great time saver for you – and it relieves pressure and stress as well – so look through your in tray and your 'to do' list.

THE CRITICAL STEPS EXPLAINED FURTHER

If you attended one of the author's workshops you would be able to practise using the framework for Handling Employees' Problems, together with the framework of Practical Leadership Skills, and to observe others doing the same – as boss and employee. You would learn much from seeing their successes and mistakes.

Something of what you would learn in a workshop is in the following pages. Questions, with explanatory comments, give more information.

1.	**Listen attentively to the employee's complaint, ensure that you fully understand it, take notes.**

This is a critical step because if you do it badly the discussion will go badly. So when someone comes along and says, 'Have you got a minute?' you need to pay attention – at once. Of course, he may not start off so helpfully, he may be much more cryptic, even offensive, and you may wonder what he wants from you.

The first twenty seconds are therefore vital because few complaints are announced as such. That's why you should move into this step whenever someone approaches you. You will notice, however, if you watch people at work or at leisure, how often they listen badly. But not you.

Over the page you will be asked to look at several ways of listening attentively. After considering each one will you then please award it points according to these ratings:

    Excellent (3 points)

    Very Good (2 points)

    Okay (1 point)

    Counter-productive (0 points)

Copyright © Russell M Tobin 2000, published by Kogan Page

Ways of listening attentively – how effective?

Excellent = 3

Very Good = 2

Okay = 1

Counter-productive = 0

	Points
1. Give the speaker your undivided attention.	
2. Don't allow yourselves to be interrupted by the telephone.	
3. Ask probing questions.	
4. Nod your head occasionally.	
5. Maintain eye contact with the speaker.	
6. Prompt the speaker with, eg, 'Go on', or 'Hm, hm', etc.	
7. Clarify what the speaker is telling you.	
8. Keep quiet while the other person is speaking.	
9. Summarize what the person has been saying.	

10. When you agree with what the employee is saying, make appropriate comments to show this.

11. Ask questions which show that you understand what the employee is saying.

12. Check your understanding of what the employee is saying.

13. Listen to what the speaker is saying without rehearsing your own answer.

14. Be seen to be taking notes of what is being said.

15. Be able to express the speaker's ideas in your own words – to his satisfaction – before you react.

As you can see, 'Listen attentively to the employee's complaint, ensure that you fully understand it, take notes' can cover a lot of ground. How you do this is up to you and on the next pages you can see the author's views on how effective the various ways are.

Comments

1. *Give the speaker your undivided attention.*

   This is something you have to *decide* to do. You may also decide to ask the employee to come back at a better time. The point is: if you are going to listen, do it well. Two points.

2. *Don't allow yourselves to be interrupted by the telephone.*

   Well, imagine sitting there with the telephone ringing, both of you driven to distraction. Explain to the caller that you are in a meeting and offer to ring back shortly. But if you can divert or hold calls so much the better. No points.

3. *Ask probing questions.*

   You probe for specifics, for facts, rather than accepting vague statements. But not too often or too quickly or you may appear to be interrogating the employee. Two points.

4. *Nod your head occasionally.*

   You appear to be following what they are saying. It encourages people to keep talking; it does *not* show that you are hearing their words. Don't let it become automatic. One point.

5. *Maintain eye contact with the speaker.*

   This shows you are more interested in the speaker than in the surroundings. But don't stare, that can be intimidating. Allow your gaze to drop to your notes once in a while. One point.

6. *Prompt the speaker with, eg, 'Go on', or 'Hm, hm', etc.*

　　This saves you having to think up questions and allows you to hear what is being said. It is also safe as you are not making any sort of comment which may be misunderstood. Two points.

7. *Clarify what the speaker is telling you.*

　　This is different to the questions in No. 3 which probe for specific information. *Clarifying*, eg, 'Do you mean...?' avoids misunderstanding. Two points.

8. *Keep quiet while the other person is speaking.*

　　And *also* when you have just asked a question. When there is silence let the employee fill it. Silence is a great tool for listening well. But it may be sensible to interrupt sometimes in order to probe or clarify. Two points.

9. *Summarize what the person has been saying.*

　　Summarizing gives you time to think. He sees you have understood. If you don't summarize you may not have understood and he'll be wondering. It is not the same as agreeing with the person. Three points.

10. *When you agree with what the employee is saying, make appropriate comments to show this.*

　　If he then looks for your constant agreement you start thinking of responses instead of listening and clarifying. Better not to make comments until you have finished Step 2. No points.

11. *Ask questions which show that you understand what the employee is saying.*

　　Asking questions *just* for that purpose could be counter-productive. Sensible questions which probe or clarify also show that you understand, but don't disrupt the flow.

12. *Check your understanding of what the employee is saying.*

    The demonstrations show this. When you check or summarize, the employee can see you are trying to understand. If you get it wrong he will put you right. Three points.

13. *Listen without rehearsing your answer.*

    Being contrary to human nature, this is hard work. But if you are rehearsing your own words, are you listening to his?

14. *Be seen to be taking notes of what is being said.*

    Taking notes does not mean that you have to be an expert shorthand writer doing 140 words per minute, nor that you slowly write down every word the employee says. It is enough to note key words:

    - which summarize a point made by you or the employee;
    - so that you can check back to see that you have dealt with these points;
    - which indicate a query you want to raise at the right moment;
    - to remind you of the key points when you follow-up later.

15. *You should be able to express his ideas in your own words – to his satisfaction – before you react.*

    Brilliant. If you can summarize like this, you've cracked it. If you *can't*, what is he to think? That you didn't hear, don't want to hear, or that you didn't understand?

> **2. Show that you understand his feelings and thank him for raising the matter.**

Understanding someone's feelings is not the same as agreeing with those feelings or condoning them. Nor is understanding enough by itself; you have to *show him* that you understand. This is something that most people do quite easily in a non-work setting. For example, when a friend complains about having to wait at the supermarket checkout you may say, 'Yes, you've got better things to do, haven't you?'

But when an employee comes along wanting your time and attention, he is not only stopping you doing what you want to do, he is probably bringing you even more work in some guise or another. And you're being asked to thank him?

However, thanking him for raising the matter can be as quick as, 'Thanks for letting me know', or 'I'm glad you've told me'. So why make a point of doing this?

Why should you thank him for raising the matter?

Comments are overleaf.

Comments

Why *should you thank him for raising the matter?*

a. When people raise a problem they could, implicitly, be attacking you. This means they may be worried about your reaction. When you thank an employee for raising the matter you are showing you do not resent him doing so.

b. If you cannot handle complaints in a positive manner, as this step indicates, people may not bring them to you. That could mean that you receive some nasty surprises from time to time because you never get early warning of problems.

c. When you say something like, 'I'm glad you let me know because...' this is a good way of moving positively into Step 3.

The Critical Steps Explained Further

You can do the second part of the step easily enough and in quite a low-key way (see the demonstrations); but what about the first part, the *empathizing*? Getting this right can be *so* useful, whilst getting it wrong or omitting it can make the employee really angry.

In showing that you understand a person's feelings, which of the following would be useful (U) and which would not be useful (Non-U)?

Useful or non-useful behaviour in empathizing?	U	Non-U
1. Show that you agree with the gist of what he is saying.		
2. Put yourself in his shoes, try to see things through his eyes and echo his feelings in your own words.		
3. Be ready to say, 'I know how you feel'.		
4. Be able to agree with the way the person feels.		
5. Ignore this step if feelings don't seem to be part of the problem. Why make heavy weather of it?		

Comments are overleaf.

Copyright © Russell M Tobin 2000, published by Kogan Page

Comments

Useful or non-useful in empathizing?

1. *Show that you agree with the gist of what he is saying.*

    Non-useful. Until you have finished Steps 1 and 2, be careful about agreeing with anything. Working through both steps gives you time to decide where you stand and, therefore, what you can support or not.

2. *Put yourself in his shoes, try to see things through his eyes and echo his feelings in your own words.*

    Very useful. This is what to do. If, in his shoes, you would have been furious, say, 'You must have been furious'. If he actually said, 'I was furious', you can echo this with, 'I'm not surprised, I would have been too'. Clues to how people feel often come out in Step 1.

3. *Be ready to say, 'I know how you feel'.*

    Ouch. Non-useful. This gets the response, 'Oh, no you don't', and an angry employee becomes more angry. Better if you can say, 'You must feel angry/upset/let down/baffled', or whatever.

4. *Be able to agree with the way the person feels.*

    Non-useful. You may understand how he feels *without in any way agreeing* with his feelings. For example, you may see that one person is angry with another. If you say he is right to be angry that may be seen as supporting him.

5. *Ignore this step if feelings don't seem to be part of the problem. Why make heavy weather of it?*

    Non-useful. This step is often important to understanding the whole problem *and* getting the employee on your side rather than possibly hostile or worried. If you feel pressurised later in the discussion it will, almost certainly, be because you missed this step. You don't have to make a big thing of it. 'You're obviously concerned', or something similar will often be enough.

3. State your own position undefensively and without hostility.

When you have understood the facts (Step 1) and the feelings (Step 2) you have the employee's side of the situation. Sometimes, although rarely, the employee will have solved his problem just by talking through it and you can stop before going into this step.

But usually he will want to know where you stand. Will you be helpful or obstructive? Will you cover up? Will you attack him? Will you make excuses or refuse to accept responsibility? Was he right to raise the problem or not?

Fortunately, by not rushing Steps 1 and 2, you have given yourself time to think. You now openly state your position in relation to the matter raised. Your position (or your stance, or where you're coming from) may be very simple, eg, 'This has to be fixed', or it may be more complex. You should state the positive aspects of your position, as well as the negative aspects. State your constraints *and* your freedom. You may express regret for the problem but this is not the same as laying blame or admitting error. In all this you have to avoid being defensive, eg, 'This isn't my fault'.

Why must you avoid being defensive?

You must also avoid hostility, eg, 'If you hadn't done such-and-such in the first place there wouldn't be a problem now'.

Why must you avoid being hostile?

Comments

You probably gave similar answers to both questions.

> Defensiveness and hostility annoy people. And they make you look bad, as if evading responsibility for the problem. The irony is that you may *not* be responsible for the problem. However, the employee has come to you wanting to find a *solution*. If you become defensive or hostile, the employee sees not a solution, but obstruction and delay.

> Defensiveness and hostility invite retaliation. If you are at fault it is better to say so, and apologise, then move forward. Otherwise you will start to make excuses as a sort of defensive armour. When that happens employees will attack the smallest chink in your defences.

> Finally, you may feel that you are not supposed to make mistakes or cause delays. True, but you're not perfect all the time and these things will happen occasionally. If you are at fault, don't cover up; own up. Then move to Step 4.

Firmness is not the same as defensiveness or hostility; sometimes you will have to state your position very firmly, eg, 'If we incur any more costs in that area we will be over budget, and we can't afford that'.

Sometimes you will use this step to *educate* the employee in safety, legislation, customer care, etc. For example, an employee (or trade union representative) says that working hours are too long in comparison with nearby businesses. Your position may be that reducing working hours without reducing associated costs (staff, heating, lighting, rent, etc) would lead to lower profit. That indicates you are not averse to shorter hours so long as profit is not affected, and to that extent you indicate that you are prepared to negotiate.

However, if you had said that shorter working hours would reduce service to your customers, and that *that* would lose business for you, this shows a firmer position and that you are not prepared to negotiate.

Sometimes you won't know where you stand on an issue, you need time to think about it. The coaching questions later will help in that case.

4. Find out if the employee has any suggestions for resolving his complaint.

This is the step that managers often leave out. In fact, anxious managers often leave out most of Step 1, all of Step 2 and all of Step 3 as well. By doing so they create pressure on themselves during the discussion and they often make work for themselves afterwards. Look at it like this:

Who has had most time to think about the problem being raised? The employee.

Who has had most time to think about a solution? The employee.

Who's had least time to think about either? You.

Quite often the person who makes a complaint will have an idea for dealing with it. 'So why didn't they make a suggestion in the first place?' you ask. The answer could well be that their experience goes somewhat as follows:

Employee: 'I've got an idea about the treacle bender, boss.'

Boss: 'Why, what's wrong with the treacle bender?' (the boss invented it and genius can't be wrong).

Employee: 'Well, it's the feed-in...'

As you see, an employee with a (hopefully) helpful idea has been turned into a complainant. In fact, for the boss there is not much difference between handling a complaint and handling a suggestion (except, possibly, bad temper and hurt feelings); the boss has moved into Step 1 of this framework.

But there is a difference for the employee between making a suggestion and making a complaint; can you note here what you think it is?

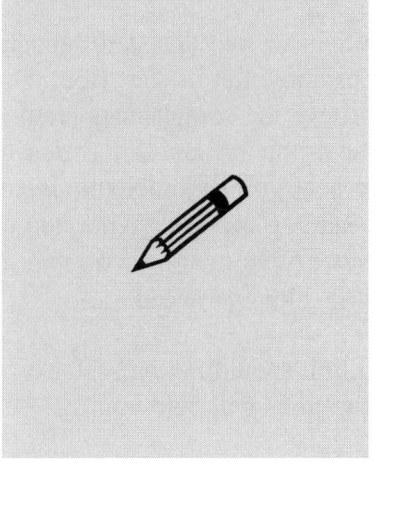

Comments

There is a difference for the employee between making a suggestion and making a complaint; what do you think it is?

> For the employee the difference is that with a suggestion he has to defend his ideas. Unless he is good at thinking through and putting forward suggestions, his natural course of action will be to make a complaint; with a complaint he is, if he wishes to be, on the attack.
>
> People invest much of their own ego in making suggestions so they think twice before they put themselves in the position of being defensive.
>
> Either way, they have to screw up the courage to say that something is wrong with the present situation, something that the boss should perhaps have realised.

So the employee has switched into the complaint mode and the boss is *inclined* to be in defensive mode. The boss, after all, has much managerial ego invested in the present system.

Even without being defensive the boss is likely to suffer from another problem that bosses sometimes have; they believe bosses ought to have solutions to all problems just because they are in the senior position.

Not true. And, although you may have a solution tucked up your sleeve, keep it there for the moment and find out if the employee has any suggestions for resolving his complaint. This can be as easy as asking, 'What do you think should be done?' Or you may have to work a little harder by asking coaching questions.

You start into this step, broadly speaking, from one of two positions. Let us start from the positive position that you believe the complaint is reasonable and that you want to see the problem fixed. First, remember that you have employees to help you fix problems. Even without an idea in your own head you can ask, 'What do you think should be done?' More often than not you will get an idea to which you can say, 'Fine, go ahead'.

If you should not be so lucky, the pages on coaching questions will help you.

The Critical Steps Explained Further

Step 4 is the coaching step. When you want to coach you usually do so by asking questions. Coaching is a really important skill which managers use to ease their own workload and to develop their people.

Coaching is not the same as training. Training is putting something into people, coaching is getting something out. Coaching is what you do:

- When you know what to do but prefer employees to learn by working through a problem themselves. They are nearer to the problem than you are and thus should devise more appropriate action programmes. You also believe employees will be more committed to their own ideas and, if they don't work, will quickly adapt them so they do work.

- When you don't know what to do about a problem and you want to start the *employee* working on it for all the reasons above.

As a general rule some coaching questions should be used before others. Will you look at those below and decide which should usually come first when you are in this step. Number it '1' and then number the remainder in what you think is their order of usefulness. Will you please briefly show your reasoning as well?

Coaching questions	Sequence	Your reasoning
'What part of your training is relevant?'		
'Have you met anything like this before?'		
'Have you any suggestions?'		
'Who could help on this?'		
'What options are there?'		

Copyright © Russell M Tobin 2000, published by Kogan Page

Comments

What is a sensible sequence in which to ask coaching questions? And what is your reasoning?

1. *'Have you any suggestions?'*

   This is, by far, the easiest question for the boss and is often the only question you need.

2. *'What options are there?'*

   If you get a negative response to No.1, this powerful follow-up question gets the employee thinking about the possibilities.

3. *'Have you met anything like this before?'*

   If No. 2 gets a poor response, this question asks employees to reflect on their experience. They may have met something sufficiently similar that gets them thinking of a solution.

4. *'What part of your training is relevant?'*

   If No. 3 reveals they have not *done* something similar, this asks if they might *know about it*. If you know about the employee's training you can focus on the relevant area.

5. *'Who could help on this?'*

   If you both lack relevant knowledge or experience, this can point the employee, and you, towards outside help.

Coaching includes having your people do things that they – and you – have never done before. At times like these you take the lead by asking the questions that get your people thinking in the right direction. This is valid even if you only ask, 'Can you come up with some ideas and we'll talk them over?' In due course you review the action eventually taken in order to learn from it.

The previous questionnaire was for when you started into this step from the position that the complaint was reasonable and you wanted to see the problem fixed.

However, your position may be that you *cannot change* whatever caused the problem for the employee. You may be able to understand that they are upset, you may be sorry they have been troubled. You may want to see them happier, but what to do?

Would it help matters if you simply said something like,

'Well, I can see you are worried, and I am sorry about that because I like to have happy employees. However, there is nothing to be done because I can't change the situation.'

Please circle one:

| It would help matters. | It would not help matters. |

What is your reasoning?

Comments are overleaf.

Comments

Your position may be that you cannot change *whatever caused the problem for the employee.*

You may be able to understand that they are upset, you may be sorry they have been troubled. You may want to see them happier, but what to do? Would it help matters if you simply said something like,

> 'Well, I can see you are worried, and I am sorry about that because I like to have happy employees. However, there is nothing to be done because I can't change the situation.'

You have only to ask how you would feel if you were shut off like that.

You would probably get all grumpy and go away muttering words like, 'We'll see about that.'

A shutout like that, besides not helping matters, does not follow Step 4; who says there is nothing to be done?

There may be occasions when you feel severely constrained but that does not mean that you cannot ask for ideas; in a difficult situation you need to keep the employee on your side. If you ask the questions right the employee may suggest things which they can do. They might also suggest things which *you* can do, such as making resources available.

How they respond will often depend on how you have handled the discussion so far; often you can really help the employee to come up with ideas.

4. *Find out if the employee has any suggestions for resolving his complaint. (continued)*

Imagine now that the employee's position (as summarized by you in Steps 1 and 2) is at *variance* with the position you stated in Step 3. On the face of it you, as a manager, are in a situation with potential for damaging your working relationship. Would you like to think for a moment and note below how you could deal with it?

When you read the section on Coaching Questions you can examine one way to deal with such a situation.

Above all, in this step avoid the temptation to show what a genius *you* are. If you provide quick answers to employee problems, you can get them coming to you with more. This step is where you seek solutions from employees by the way you ask coaching questions.

You have to recognize a coaching opportunity when it comes along and thus develop your people; how do you *know* something is outside their experience or, indeed, beyond their imagination?

On the other hand, remember that this is a framework. If an inexperienced employee comes to you with a technical problem it may be more sensible to give a quick answer and let them learn from applying it.

When they come up with ideas that are only partly right, you can build on those ideas with 'Yes, and...' The whole idea is that you should not rush too quickly into the next step.

> **5. If applicable, specify what you will do to correct the situation.**

'If applicable...'

And *only* if applicable. It is better if people can solve their own problems: better for their self-esteem, for their self-development, and for your workload! Any action you do take will stem from your position, eg your desire to see the problem fixed. Sometimes you will want to take some action even if the employee does not suggest it, because something is clearly your responsibility (or a real hot issue) and you cannot delegate it.

'specify what you will do...'

This may be easy, eg 'I'll ask Payroll what happened to your overtime'. If you are more vague, like 'looking into' something, you may not set a specific follow-up date (Practical Leadership Skill 7).

However, when you do set a specific follow-up date, in order to report back, this ensures nothing is 'swept under the carpet' – where it might fester! A specific follow-up date shows commitment, and you won't like to report back without some progress to show.

'to correct the situation.'

Usually you will be trying to bring the problem to an end without delay. Beware of prolonging it or putting it to one side. It is easy to say, 'Leave it with me', and then let things slide. If you want it left with you to think about, you should remember that often the employee can think about it just as well as you.

If your position is that a work problem *must* be fixed then you should follow-up on it. Also ask yourself if the action planned will really correct the situation.

It may be, of course, that your position was that the employee would have to live with the situation, in which case you would have explained why.

Remember, *only* if applicable.

There may be more to a situation than a discussion between you and one employee. For example, an employee coming to you with a complaint on behalf of work colleagues will have to report back. How much better it will be if they can say what action *they* will be taking (this also gives them some control and some responsibility). And, if they report that *you* are going to be doing something, how much more convincing if they can give a follow-up date.

One specific thing you can sometimes do, to correct a situation, is to represent people's views up the line, again with a specific follow-up date to report back.

While it is occasionally appropriate for you to do something to correct the situation, it usually creates additional work for you. However, in many cases, giving your approval to suggestions from the employee will be all the action you need take.

You can also delegate to the employee something you might do yourself. As an example take, 'I'll ask Payroll what happened to your overtime'. This could involve you in a lengthy visit or a long phone call to Payroll Department. Instead, you could ring them and arrange for your employee to visit them. This brings your authority into play but saves you some work – and Payroll have to deal directly with their complaining customer.

A WORD ON ASSERTIVENESS

When people seek your help, it is very easy to promise it – and then fail to deliver. On those occasions everyone loses and your reputation suffers too.

To avoid that trap you need to assert your right to say 'No' – and not feel bad about it. Step 3 can help you. Here are some examples of stating your position undefensively:

- 'I'd like to help but I don't want to make promises I can't keep.'

- 'I'd like to help but with my other priorities I'd only let you down.'

- 'I have so much to do that I can't even think of offering help.'

- 'My position is that I only make promises I can keep, so I can't help this time.'

- 'It certainly needs fixing but I just don't have the time to be the fixer.'

You won't feel badly about using such phrases with staff, and with colleagues, *provided* you add another phrase such as, 'But what other options do you have?' or, 'Perhaps Ronnie could help'. At that point, you help the other person to go away with some plan that costs you nothing.

What handy phrases have you noticed other people using effectively? And what phrases work for you already? Please note here those you feel comfortable with yourself.

HOW YOU CAN GO WRONG

While the demonstrations show how to get it right, it is useful to know some ways in which things can go wrong.

1. Listen attentively to the employee's complaint, ensure that you fully understand it, take notes.

- Someone may come to you in a blazing temper, or in a really distressed condition, pouring out words and emotion. If you say, 'Calm down', you are likely to get a bad reaction ('Whaddya mean, calm down?').

    People are *entitled* to be emotional so it is better to just listen, pick out what you can and ask questions if appropriate. Once they see you listening well, they will respond well and calm down.

- In similar vein, if someone gives you a lot of verbal abuse, you *could* respond, 'Don't talk to me like that'. But that doesn't advance the discussion. Work through Step 1 and Step 2.

    If you don't get the chance to understand and empathize then follow the framework into Step 3. State your position, undefensively and without hostility, as, 'I want to see this sorted out but I can't do anything until I understand the problem'. Then go back to Step 1 with 'Tell me about it'.

2. Show that you understand his feelings and thank him for raising the matter.

- You may miss this step completely if you are frantically thinking what to do (which is Step 5 and not necessary yet). If you therefore propose action without having fully understood the problem (because *feelings* are part of the problem) the employee could be very short with you.

- As you listen attentively in Step 1, you will hear words and expressions that you can reflect back in Step 2. Even if you get this wrong they can see that you are, at the very least, trying to understand how they feel.

3. State your own position undefensively and without hostility.

- You can get hung up because you feel you would look weak if you deviated from your stated position.

  Sometimes it will be sensible to hold firm but at other times you will hear points of view in Step 4 that cause you to modify your position. You don't have to say, 'I am willing to change my position' (though sometimes it might help). It will be evident as you accept employee suggestions that are not fully compatible with your original position. But careful, it could also mean you are too easily persuaded.

- You may fail to state your position fully. Then, when the employee makes suggestions in Step 4, you have to turn them down. The wrong suggestions come up because the employee does not know the limits within which they must work. Which is because you didn't explain them in stating your position. Thus they become angry because they think you are not being open and above board.

4. Find out if the employee has any suggestions for resolving his complaint.

- Instead of practising fire-prevention it's all too easy to practise fire-fighting and, of course, it's more exciting. What happens is that the employee deals with a problem and then complains about it. The boss follows Step 1, Step 2 and Step 3 ('We certainly don't want that happening and I'm glad you fixed it'). Then he thinks that Step 4 and Step 5 don't apply. So he says, 'Thanks very much' and ends the discussion.

  Unfortunately the employee knows the problem will happen again and probably has ideas for preventing that – if only you would ask. He goes away dissatisfied, and you wonder why he seems so grumpy.

  Always ask yourself if you should be looking at future prevention. If so, then move into Step 4 with, 'And we don't want to see it happening again so have you any ideas?' Or something similar.

- You may have asked for ideas, failed to get any, and started to push your own idea for what the employee should do. The employee finds fault with your idea and you then feel pressured to come up with more ideas.

    This problem will occur more with an experienced employee than a learner. You avoid it by working hard at getting suggestions from the employee. Only bring in your own ideas if necessary and then ask for the employee's opinion, eg, 'How would it be if...?'

- Employees may come to you too often with smallish problems. They take up your time and the employees appear not to be self-reliant.

    This can happen if you are too quick to provide solutions. If the solutions are so easy, try turning them into questions. This will get your people thinking for themselves. Soon they will stop coming with little problems and, with bigger ones, they will come with proposals for solutions.

5. If applicable, specify what you will do to correct the situation.

- Promising to do something, and then failing to do it because of pressure of other work, is bad for everyone.

    The solution is easy. Be prepared to say that you cannot help. Don't make promises you can't keep.

- Taking a task from an employee when you *know* it is their work, but you think they are too busy, can also let you down.

    Being too nice to them can be nasty for you. You still have pressure of your own work so why not delegate the task to another employee who is not so busy? (But if you do that often you should consider the effect it might have on teamwork.)

- You can put yourself under awful pressure by thinking that *you* have to find a solution.

    Taking from employees the task of thinking is something you should not do. That's bad for them.

Notes

COACHING QUESTIONS

You can check your thinking, and your understanding of the preceding material, through the Coaching Questions that follow. Comments are given after each page so please write your own answers before turning over. You will also gain further understanding through trying out the steps later and reflecting on what happened when you did.

| 1. | **Listen attentively to the employee's complaint, ensure that you fully understand it, take notes.** |

You are sitting in your office, grafting away, when one of your people flings open the door and comes crashing in. He is clearly in a towering rage, his opening words are angry, loud and abusive. You feel offended and under attack. What do you do?

Take a minute to think about your answer and then tick one or more of the following.

	Your options	Your choice
a.	Stand up and shout him down. (He shouldn't be talking to the boss in that manner.)	
b.	Remain seated and, in a quiet voice, tell him to calm down.	
c.	Remain seated and, in a quiet voice, say that you want him to come back when he has calmed down and you will readily listen to his problem then.	
d.	Ask him to tell you what is the matter.	
e.	Your own option:	

Comments are overleaf.

Copyright © Russell M Tobin 2000, published by Kogan Page

Comments

You were in your office when you were assailed by a very angry employee and had to decide what to do. Which option did you choose?

a. *Stand up and shout him down. (He shouldn't be talking to the boss in that manner.)*

   This sounds like a good way to heart failure for one of you, if not both. It holds up the discussion while you indulge yourself instead of moving it forward.

b. *Remain seated and, in a quiet voice, tell him to calm down.*

   This might lead to, 'Whaddya mean, calm down? I'm *!*!* angry.' This could lead to you making the response in (c).

c. *Remain seated and, in a quiet voice, say that you want him to come back when he has calmed down and you will readily listen to his problem then.*

   You still have yourself under control, well done, but have you moved things forward? The employee *still* needs to vent his or her anger. If he can't do it with you he might go and do it elsewhere – with unfortunate results.

d. *Ask him to tell you what is the matter.*

   Letting him see that you want to listen now is a very positive way of calming people down. He will talk more coherently too. This is the only response that gets a tick.

e. *Your own option:*

   How does it stand up in light of the above?

2. Show that you understand his feelings and thank him for raising the matter.

Feelings can be more or less important, depending on the circumstances. In fact, the complaint itself can sometimes seem really trivial whilst the emotions generated by the problem are enormously powerful.

Think of your own experience, or of someone you know, and write a few words in response to these questions.

1. Suppose you felt really strongly about something, and you let your feelings show in words or actions. How would you then feel if your boss did not react to your feelings?	
2. Suppose you felt strongly about something, but *concealed* your feelings. How would you feel if your boss still didn't identify those feelings – *even though* you had concealed them?	
3. What could be the likely consequences if your boss did not *show* that he understood your feelings?	
4. You are listening to someone and you can understand *what* he is saying. However, although he clearly wants some understanding from you, you can't understand *why* he is saying it. What do you do?	

Comments

You were asked to write a few words about feelings.

1. *Suppose you felt really strongly about something, and you let your feelings show in words or actions. How would you then feel if your boss did not react to your feelings?*

   When people feel strongly about something, their emotions are a large part of the message they are sending. If your boss failed to *show* understanding of your feelings you would probably feel frustrated. Also, the boss would not understand the whole problem, and may therefore try to solve the wrong problem.

2. *Suppose you felt strongly about something, but* concealed *your feelings. How would you feel if your boss still didn't identify those feelings – even though you had concealed them?*

   Paradoxically, you may feel disappointed with the boss's poor powers of perception. If he did try to understand your feelings you may give further information – which would reveal the total problem to be solved.

3. *What could be the likely consequences if your boss did* not show *that he understood your feelings?*

   You lose some communication and a chance for co-operation. You may also lose some respect for the boss.

4. *You are listening to someone and you can understand what he is saying. However, although he clearly wants some understanding from you, you can't understand why he is saying it. What do you do?*

   You cannot 'show that you understand his feelings...'. So why not ask, 'How do you feel about this?'

   This will get you an informative answer that allows you to assess the seriousness of the situation. Then you can show the concern that the employee needs to see.

Empathizing is not the same as sympathizing and the difference can be important. With sympathy you may identify too closely with a person and his emotions. Empathy is *understanding* emotions without becoming emotional yourself.

Here are a few examples of feelings shown by an employee giving information in Step 1. Then there are some alternative responses.

In each pair of responses, which one is empathy (E), that is retaining objectivity, and which one is sympathy (S), which can cause you to lose objectivity?

The feelings shown	Alternative responses	E or S
1. 'I tripped over and they all laughed at me. I felt an absolute fool.'	a. 'I would have given them a piece of my mind.' b. 'You were embarrassed in front of all those people?'	
2. 'It's just not good enough.'	a. 'I don't think so either.' b. 'You're fed up with it, are you?'	
3. 'That machine is downright dangerous.'	a. 'You're worried about your safety?' b. 'Yes, it should have been thrown out ages ago.'	

Comments are overleaf.

Copyright © Russell M Tobin 2000, published by Kogan Page

Comments

You were asked to distinguish between examples of empathy and sympathy.

1. *'I tripped over and they all laughed at me. I felt an absolute fool.'*

   Alternative (a), *'I would have given them a piece of my mind'*, is sympathy. It does not help the employee to 'dump' his emotions and be ready to go positive on solving the problem.

   Alternative (b), *'You were embarrassed in front of all those people?'*, is empathy. Now that someone else can see how he felt, the employee can start to think about dealing with the problem.

2. *'It's just not good enough.'*

   Alternative (a), *'I don't think so either'*, is sympathy. Boss and employee sit together and agree, 'Ain't it awful', but it doesn't move things forward.

   Alternative (b), *'You're fed up with it, are you?'*, is empathy. Here the employee can say, 'Yes, I am', and know the boss understands.

3. *'That machine is downright dangerous.'*

   Alternative (a), *'You're worried about your safety?'*, is empathy. This becomes the problem to agree on and then solve.

   Alternative (b), *'Yes, it should have been thrown out ages ago'*, is sympathy. But it wasn't thrown out. And if it isn't thrown out now, is anything to be done about keeping the employee safe?

Here are three more examples of feelings shown by an employee giving information in Step 1. Then there are the alternative responses.

In each pair of responses, which one is empathy (E), that is retaining objectivity, and which one is sympathy (S), which can cause you to lose objectivity?

The feelings shown	Alternative responses	E or S
4. 'This should not keep happening in a decent organization.'	a. 'They'll never get their act together, this lot.' b. 'This is the last straw, is it?'	
5. 'I think it is appalling.'	a. 'I'm not surprised you're upset.' b. 'You're dead right, it is.'	
6. 'The lads are moaning about their bonus.'	a. 'Yeah, they're out for all they can get.' b. 'Giving you a hard time, are they?'	

Comments are overleaf.

Copyright © Russell M Tobin 2000, published by Kogan Page

Comments

You were asked to distinguish between empathy and sympathy, with three more examples.

4. *'This should not keep happening in a decent organization.'*

    Alternative (a), *'They'll never get their act together, this lot'*, is sympathy. This is a useless remark and hardly offers sympathy either.

    Alternative (b), *'This is the last straw, is it?'*, is empathy. Perhaps it is not the last straw but boss and employee can now move forward to remove the cause of the problem – if that meets with the boss's position.

5. *'I think it is appalling.'*

    Alternative (a), *'I'm not surprised you're upset'*, is empathy. Having had his feelings recognized, the employee is then ready to join with the boss in problem-solving.

    Alternative (b), *'You're dead right, it is'*, is sympathy. This can lead to trouble if it undermines the boss's position. It lets the employee in with, 'So what are you going to do about it?'; pressure the boss can do without.

6. *'The lads are moaning about their bonus.'*

    Alternative (a), *'Yeah, they're out for all they can get'*, is sympathy. Again the boss is joining in the 'Ain't it awful' game. These are thoughtless words without action or help.

    Alternative (b), *'Giving you a hard time, are they?'*, is empathy. This is from Demonstration 3 and it lets the boss focus on the real problem which the employee must solve.

| 3. | State your own position undefensively and without hostility. |

In order to know your position when others need a lead, you should have good knowledge about your job and your specialization, about your organization's values, objectives and policies, about relevant legislation, and so on.

Without getting into the small detail of complaints, how are you on the core values of your organization? Try to describe below the core value or belief that would guide you in each of the following circumstances.

1. Someone coming with a complaint about health and safety.
2. Someone needing extra income and asking for a rise or for overtime.
3. Someone who feels another member of the team is not pulling his weight.

Comments are overleaf.

Comments

What you wrote should generally have answered the following questions in a positive way.

1. *Someone coming with a complaint about health and safety.*

    Are people entitled to have a safe place of work?

    Are employees aware of their personal responsibilities for health and safety?

    Do you do everything that is reasonably practicable to keep people safe?

2. *Someone needing extra income and asking for a rise or for overtime.*

    Should you manufacture overtime if it is not needed?

    As a general rule, should you give someone a rise in isolation from others?

    Do you have a system for assessing performance?

3. *Someone who feels another member of the team is not pulling his weight.*

    As a general rule should some team members gain at the expense of others?

    Are team members encouraged, and trained if necessary, to be open with each other?

    Are you able to assess how individuals are performing within a team?

    Are you ready to give recognition for dependable work?

    And to deal promptly with unacceptable performance?

There are three more sets of circumstances on the next page.

Still on the core values of your organization. Try to describe below the core value or belief that would guide you in each of the following circumstances.

4. Someone who complains that his job is getting harder and harder to handle.
5. A manager who complains that the union is blocking essential change.
6. Someone who complains about discrimination or harassment on grounds of race, sex, age or disability.

Comments are overleaf.

Comments

Again, what you wrote should generally have answered the following questions in a positive way.

4. *Someone who complains that his job is getting harder and harder to handle.*

   Should people be trained and/or coached for new tasks?

   Should people have help when they need it?

   Do you have ways, however crude, of assessing the workload of your employees?

5. *A manager who complains that the union is blocking essential change.*

   Should people be consulted about changes that effect their work? Should their views be sought – and taken into account?

   Should union members and officials be specific about the problems they foresee? And be expected to contribute to solving them?

   Can an essential change be allowed *not* to happen?

6. *Someone who complains about discrimination or harassment on grounds of race, sex, age or disability.*

   Do you have clear written policies on these matters?

   Are these followed in the spirit of the policies as well as to the letter of them?

   If there are no written policies, have you made clear that what counts is ability and that you will stand no nonsense either way?

Sometimes you won't know where you stand on an issue, you need time to think about it or to consult someone else about it.

If that happens, how could you state your position undefensively and without hostility? Note the words you would use to avoid appearing hostile or defensive.

Sometimes you may find yourself in a negotiating situation. Once you have stated your position, should you be prepared to change it? If so, to what extent?

Comments are on the next page.

Comments

The questions asked about your certainty regarding your position.

Sometimes you won't know where you stand on an issue, you need time to think about it or to consult someone else about it. If that happens, how would you state your position undefensively and without hostility?

Your position is that you don't know what your position is, so how about,

> 'I'm not sure what to say on this, I need to think about it (and perhaps talk with Fred).'

That's nice and open, and absolutely honest. It's better than getting yourself into trouble with lies or obfuscation. And you still have Step 4 to come.

Sometimes you may find yourself in a negotiating situation. Once you have stated your position, should you be prepared to change it? If so, to what extent?

An awkward question until you remember that your position is where you stand in light of all the knowledge, experience, policy, and philosophy you have.

It is where you are coming from, your starting point, and you are almost certainly open to new ideas that *could* cause you to change your position.

But they may need to be very powerful ideas to cause that change. Any moves away from your original position should be checked against the reason for it. You can see, in the demonstrations, how your position works for you.

You can see how you make time to think by working well through Steps 1 and 2 – and how this helps you to avoid a big mistake here.

> Their facts and feelings + your position
> =
> a joint platform for moving forward.

Now and again someone will complain to you about a policy which is perceived as unfair. And *you* may perceive it as unfair.

Below are three different ways of stating your position. How would you rate their effectiveness – as a long-term personal style of leadership?

Give each one points out of 10.

	'My position is...'	Points
A.	'*They say* that is what we have to do, so that's the policy.'	
B.	'That's the agreed policy, and I may not be happy about it, but I've explained it and, until it's changed, that is what I am paid to implement.'	
C.	'That's the policy, and I may not be happy about it, but it's agreed. I've explained it and I am working to change it but, until it's changed, that is what I am paid to implement.'	

Comments are overleaf.

Comments

'My position is...'

A. *'They say that is what we have to do, so that's the policy.'*

This statement implies that you may prefer a different policy. It could be taken as weakness, the employee thinking you may not support the official position. If you hint that you are weak about your position (not the same as being unsure of it) you may come under pressure.

Low score.

B. *'That's the agreed policy, and I may not be happy about it, but I've explained it and, until it's changed, that is what I am paid to implement.'*

If you are not happy with a policy you can still say something like this. Then you can move the discussion forward into Step 4.

This can be useful with someone who thinks your participative management style permits him not to follow policy unless he gets a direct order ('Do it, or else'). You may not relish that sort of power display but this tip has the same effect as a direct order.

Medium/high score.

C. *'That's the policy, and I may not be happy about it, but it's agreed. I've explained it and I am working to change it but, until it's changed, that is what I am paid to implement.'*

This is similar to B but you have the best of both worlds, ie working for an alternative whilst being relatively comfortable with applying present policy.

Higher score.

B and C show realism about who finances the lifestyle of yourself and your family.

| 4. | Find out if the employee has any suggestions for resolving his complaint. |

Here are some ways of finding out if the employee has any suggestions for resolving his complaint. Which do you think are good ways (G) and which are not so good (NSG)? Please tick in the appropriate column.

Good ways or not so good?	G	NSG
1. Ask what the employee has done so far to solve the problem.		
2. Unless the problem needs an urgent solution, leave the employee to think about it for a while.		
3. If you don't get acceptable ideas quickly just tell the employee what to do.		
4. Refer back to specific problems which you noted from Step 1 and ask, one at a time, how each can be handled.		
5. Restate in different words the problem to be solved and ask again for suggestions.		
6. Having sought ideas, be ready to shift your position and negotiate in response to them.		

Comments are overleaf.

Comments

Good ways or not so good ways of finding out if the employee has any suggestions for resolving his complaint?

1. *Ask what the employee has done so far to solve the problem.*

   Good. As he describes what has been done so far, this triggers off thoughts about what else can be done. If he has done nothing, it is a face-saver that assumes that he does have ideas – and some will now come.

2. *Unless the problem needs an urgent solution, leave the employee to think about it for a while.*

   Good. If neither of you has any ideas, this is always good practice. Why not adjourn?

3. *If you don't get acceptable ideas quickly just tell the employee what to do.*

   Not so good. Usually this is okay only if the employee is still learning about whatever caused the problem and you are in a training mode. But this will seldom be the case.

4. *Refer back to specific problems which you noted from Step 1 and ask, one at a time, how each can be handled.*

   Good. This breaks down the overall problem into its component parts and each part becomes more manageable.

5. *Restate in different words the problem to be solved and ask again for suggestions.*

   Good. For example, suppose 'How can you get there?' receives a 'Dunno'. Now change that to, 'What transport is available?' and you might get, 'Well, there are buses...'

6. *Having sought ideas, be ready to shift your position and negotiate in response to them.*

   This could be either or both. Often you *have* to stick to your position – unless you rushed into it. Most of the time you should get him to make suggestions based on your position.

Let us look at the important switch from Step 3 to Step 4. Imagine, if you would, a specific complaint.

> In a pub the floor covering behind the bar counter has worn out. An employee has tripped because of it. The employee nearly suffered injury and felt foolish in front of customers. When the employee complained, the manager understood the incident and the embarrassment (Steps 1 and 2). Although concerned about safety, the manager stated his position, in Step 3, as being that there is no money to replace the floor covering.

The manager next made one or more of the following statements, *alone or in combination*. Which of these statements is/are most likely to be effective in getting suggestions and reaching a solution? Please note your thoughts at the end, then see the next page for comments.

1.	'I'm afraid we're stuck with it. You'll just have to be extra careful.'
2.	'We ought to do something, what do you think?'
3.	'We can't spend any money but you still have to be safe.'
4.	'I don't suppose you have any ideas, have you?'
5.	'Any ideas for fixing it?'
6.	'I know there's nothing in the budget for repairs but let me try the Area Manager next time he comes.'
Your views on the above:	

Comments

The best combination, in switching from Step 3 to Step 4, is Statement 3 combined with Statement 5. Next comes No. 2.

1. *'I'm afraid we're stuck with it. You'll just have to be extra careful.'*

   That is a shutout showing that the boss, being without ideas himself, believes that no one else can have any ideas either. It is counter-productive.

2. *'We ought to do something, what do you think?'*

   This implies concern about safety, but only weakly. But the manager is big enough to ask for ideas, despite (apparently) having none himself.

3. *'We can't spend any money but you still have to be safe.'*

   This restates his position on money and repeating, '...you still have to be safe', shows determination not to put the employee at risk.

4. *'I don't suppose you have any ideas, have you?'*

   This suggests that the boss expects no ideas (and perhaps wants no ideas). It sets the mood for the boss to find problems with any ideas that do come up. It also seems that, without ideas, the employee would still be expected to take the risk.

5. *'Any ideas for fixing it?'*

   This joins with Statement 3. Any ideas must be no-cost and must give safety; no half measures. The employee will have at least two useful responses.

6. *'I know there's nothing in the budget for repairs but let me try the Area Manager next time he comes.'*

   This is another abdication of responsibility. It's the same as saying, 'I don't think I'll get any money when I ask but keep on taking the risk until I can confirm that.'

> Statements 3 and 5 focus on the problem to be solved.
>
> As you can see from statements 1, 4 and 6, it is too easy to move into Step 4 in a negative way.

4. *Find out if the employee has any suggestions for resolving his complaint. (continued)*

Now and again you will hear some ideas that you don't like. If that happens you must take care that your own response does not demotivate the employee.

Some employee ideas may not relate to the problem at all, or may go outside the parameters set by the boss in his position, or the ideas seem to be unworkable. Below are some 'boss responses' to such unwelcome ideas. They relate to the example of the employee in the pub where there is no money to fix the dangerous floor covering behind the bar.

Of these responses, which are likely to have a positive effect (P) by moving the discussion forward? Which are likely to have a negative effect (N) by stopping or holding back the discussion? Please mark accordingly.

Positive and negative boss responses to unwelcome suggestions	P or N
1. 'I'm afraid I can't see that working.'	
2. 'Yes, I see. What do you think that might cost?'	
3. 'Have you no better ideas than that?'	
4. 'That sounds okay, how would you go about it?'	
5. 'Okaaay... any other ideas?'	
6. 'How will that make things safer?'	
7. 'Can you think of any other options?'	

Comments are overleaf.

Copyright © Russell M Tobin 2000, published by Kogan Page

Comments

What was the effect of the boss responses to the employee's ideas regarding the dangerous pub floor?

1. *'I'm afraid I can't see that working.'*

    Negative. This doesn't move the discussion forward. Better to use No. 5 or No. 7 below.

2. *'Yes, I see. What do you think that might cost?'*

    Positive. Not agreeing or denying. Showing again that the boss has money constraints. If the idea costs money the employee may now come up with a no-cost idea.

3. *'Have you no better ideas than that?'*

    Negative. Destructive. People won't come up with ideas if they get this sort of response. Questions that focus on the problems to be solved are better.

4. *'That sounds okay, how would you go about it?'*

    Positive. A coaching question asking for more detail, so the boss can 'ensure that the employee has an appropriate action programme'.

5. *'Okaaay... any other ideas?'*

    Positive. This shows that the idea has been heard – but not welcomed. Asking for more ideas should let the unwelcome one fall away – but without criticizing it.

6. *'How will that make things safer?'*

    Positive. This is a coaching question asking the employee to expand on his idea. If it does make things safer, he can say how. If it doesn't, he can drop it and come up with something else.

7. *'Can you think of any other options?'*

    Positive. Much the same as No. 5 above. The word 'options' suggests that more than one idea is possible.

5. If applicable, specify what you will do to correct the situation.

Sometimes you will take some action yourself – perhaps because the employee suggested it – but you should always decide if you can delegate that action to the employee. Why? As an effective manager you will not want to do something which your people could do. You may have to train, or coach them, to do it but once they have learned they can do it again, and again, and again. This leaves you to get on with the things that *only you* can do.

Use this principle right now. Take a few minutes to review the last two working weeks. (Your in tray, your 'pending' tray, your diary and your 'to do' list will help.) Look for the things you promised to do after employees came with problems. Look at where you said, 'Leave it with me', or 'I'll have a word with them', or 'Let me think about it'.

Please list those tasks below. Then note the person to whom you could delegate each task if you really tried. If you think you can't delegate a task, please show the reason in the second column instead.

Use the third column to estimate the time you will save for yourself if you delegate those tasks.

The tasks	Delegate to	Saving

Comments are overleaf.

Comments

In examining your trays, your diary and your 'to do' list you may, like many managers, have found several commit-ments to do things for employees. You may also have included other tasks which did *not* come from employees but which you should delegate anyway.

Whatever the number of tasks you noted, there is a fair chance that you had not done some by the time you promised you would. Is that right, is some employee still awaiting a promised response from his boss? Circle one:

YES   NO

If the answer is 'No', pat yourself on the back.

Even if there is only one delayed item on the list, consider the effect that your unintended delay may have on your employee. What is the effect *on you* if your boss promises to do something and fails to deliver? Note the effect here.

> What tasks of your own could you delegate?
> List those on the previous page also, with the time you will save.

Comment

> If the matter was important you may become frustrated if your boss doesn't deliver the action promised. You will start to wish you had never gone to the boss in the first place and your respect for the boss may be diminished. You can feel demotivated. Serious stuff.

This is why you take action only 'if applicable'. There are two major pay-offs:

- You don't do things you needn't do. You can use your valuable time to better effect. By delegation alone some managers have saved themselves up to seven hours a week.

- You don't hold up your employees through procrastination.

And there is a third pay-off; you develop your people.

5. *If applicable, specify what you will do to correct the situation. (continued)*

This business of not picking up work that you shouldn't is really important. These questions will help you see why.

1. Leave aside for a moment the issue of complaints. Think of other situations where employees come to you for advice, or for you to do something for them.

   Have you ever done for others something that they *could* do, because you can do it better?

   What is the effect on your workload?

   What is the effect on them if you delay handling their problems?

2. Have you ever known a boss or team leader who let promised action slide, possibly in the hope that the problems would go away?

   How did that influence the way other people viewed that boss?

3. You have examined the consequences of taking on work that you shouldn't, and of doing work that you should delegate. As a result, are there any colleagues or employees with whom you really must be more assertive in declining to take on work?

Comments

1. *Leave aside for a moment the issue of complaints. Think of other situations where employees come to you for advice, or for you to do something for them.*

   Have you ever done for others something that they could do, *because you can do it better?*

   What is the effect on your workload?

   What is the effect on them if you delay handling their problems?

   If ever you find yourself saying words like, 'Leave it with me', or, 'Let me think about it', you are probably creating more work for yourself. At the same time you cause delay for your employees – delay that can demotivate them.

   They also may wonder why you take ages to do something that they could do quickly if you just gave them the right guidance – which often will need to be very little.

2. *Have you ever known a boss or team leader who let promised action slide, possibly in the hope that the problems would go away? How did that influence the way other people viewed that boss?*

   The boss might simply not have had the time to do the promised work, but people don't know that and it can be demotivating.

   If it happens to you, try to ensure you get a follow-up date before you leave something with that sort of boss – but *must* you leave it with him?

3. *You have examined the consequences of taking on work that you shouldn't, and of doing work that you should delegate. As a result, are there any colleagues or employees with whom you really must be more assertive in declining to take on work?*

   Remember that delegation helps to develop your staff, and frees you up for more important work, for time to develop yourself, and for a better home life.

   You may like to look back to page 80 for a word on assertiveness.

EXCEPTIONAL SITUATIONS

'Yes, but...?' and 'What if...?'

If you think the demonstrations seemed to go well, you have to remember:

ACTION ➡ ➡ ➡ REACTION

- If people are handled well they usually respond well.
- If you listen well they'll talk.
- If you don't listen well they'll stop talking.
- If you stay positive it is hard for them to be negative.
- If you are rational they soon stop being irrational.
- If you ask for ideas you will usually get them.

And the whole thrust of this framework, with the framework for Practical Leadership Skills in the background, is positive.

However, there are exceptions, some situations can be difficult. You may have your own way of handling them but the examples in the following pages are based on the two frameworks shown in this workbook.

Some pleasant exceptions are included as well.

1. 'What if I can't meet their needs?'

You may have looked at the demonstration on giving notice (page 21) and thought that the boss had an easy solution in being able to offer more work, and thus more money. What if she had not been able to do that?

To answer that question check the demonstration against the framework. Step 1 would have been much the same. Also Step 2 and Step 3. But the boss's position would also have included something like, 'But I can't see any way to increase your hours, not at this time anyway.'

Then the boss goes into Step 4 with much the same words as in the demonstration. And she hopes, really hopes, for some ideas from Lisa. At least Lisa now knows that the boss wants her to stay; she may previously have been unsure.

In Step 5 all the boss may be able to say is that she will look for opportunities to increase Lisa's hours, and it is quite possible that she will find one or two.

But if you can't meet the employee's needs then you can't.

2. 'What if I can't agree with the complaint?'

You can give yourself a problem if you try to get too quickly into Step 3 by stating your disagreement. That can lead to a heated argument before you have fully understood the complaint or the feelings behind it.

Give yourself thinking time by working through Steps 1 and 2. Look at the demonstration on fire danger as an example (page 35). If the boss thought there was *not* a fire hazard, Step 1 would hardly change. There would have been understanding and thanks in Step 2, but no agreement.

Step 3 would then be something like, 'I certainly want a safe exit in case of fire but I think there's plenty of space for people to get through. However, (Step 4 now) if you can think of an easy way to make more space I'm happy to listen.' Now, if the employee's ideas involve trouble or expense they are simply, 'Not worth the bother.'

If the employee doesn't like your non-acceptance, the discussion can be brought to an end by setting a follow-up date: 'If the situation changes for the worse then by all means come to me again.' Thus the employee can raise the matter again if the situation deteriorates. At the same time the boss, alerted to the potential risk, may inspect the area more often.

3. 'What if you need to check out the facts first?'

This is a question you might ask after the building site demonstration. Look back to that on page 29.

The boss's position was that he didn't want the Foreman to be held up, nor to have aggravation. You don't require any more facts to say this sort of thing, it is true all the time.

The need to get someone else's story does not stop you asking for ideas in Step 4 of the framework. But be careful about what you commit yourself to in Step 5. Look at the dialogue in the same demonstration on page 32.

4. 'Yes, but people still keep coming with problems.'

This may be because they are accustomed to a sympathetic hearing followed by the boss taking on the problem. Or they like the status that comes with having time with the boss.

Work at using Step 4 well so that they eventually learn to come with problems wrapped in solutions.

5. 'Yes, but some of my people are really overloaded.'

After someone makes a complaint you won't like sending them away with additional work when you believe they already have more than enough. So you take it on instead. But if they are really overloaded, which of these is better for you both?

(a) You take on the work and delay it and the employee carries on being overloaded?

(b) You use your time to manage things so that the employee *can* cope?

The choice is obvious. Your time can then be used to coach the employee to work on time management techniques, setting priorities, work measurement and use of resources.

6. 'If I change my position won't I look an easy touch?'

If that thought stops you stating your position you will appear to be prevaricating, on the defensive, and inviting hostility.

Some of the time, with work problems, it won't matter too much how you state your position. It is hard to have a well-thought-out position on everything. What you *can* have is a *tentative* position which leads smoothly from Step 3 into Step 4. Here are some examples of stating your position in a tentative way.

- 'We ought to do something about this (but I'm not sure what).'

- 'I can't say this problem is a high priority (but I'm not ignoring it).'

- 'On the face of it, it can't be right (but I'm not too sure).'

If you add to each of those sentences the words, 'But what do you suggest should be done?' this starts you into Step 4 and you are seen to be not evading the issue.

It is at this point that you have to handle any ideas well. You should go along with suggestions unless there is a good reason not to. If there is such a reason, this becomes part of your position and will help you to firm it up. You can then state it more positively and ask for ideas based on your joint situations (Step 1 + Step 2 + Step 3).

It would be unfortunate if you stated a position you cannot sustain. Or if you promise in Step 5 to do something which is not based on a sound position.

7. 'Won't I look stupid if I don't have a solution?'

You can feel pressured, especially when the employee says, 'What are you going to do then?' However, you'll look more stupid if you jump too quickly to a solution that turns out to be wrong. You will also lose respect if you don't ask the employee for his ideas.

Don't be afraid of not having a solution. Remember Practical Leadership Skill No. 5 (Allow the employee adequate time to think through the problem and to suggest a solution). New problems are often just as new to you as to the employee, but it is still true that they are nearer to their problems than you are.

8. 'Yes, but one employee won't take "No" for an answer.'

Some people are like that.

Just follow the framework. Move from Step 3, where the employee is arguing against your position, into Step 4. This will get them thinking as they try to suggest things that will get them their own way.

What you do then, is ask the employee how his suggestions relate to your position. You can keep on restating your position and asking for ideas that will fit with it – and with the problem you defined in Steps 1 and 2.

9. 'Yes, but I've heard some really stupid ideas.'

They may sound stupid to you but perhaps they don't seem so to the employee. This can happen if you have not explained your position, and the employee thus has no parameters within which to make acceptable suggestions.

Look back to page 44 where the boss seeks ideas for the employee keeping himself safe.

You can simply ignore the daft ideas and ask for more. The bad ones then tend to fall away.

Copyright © Russell M Tobin 2000, published by Kogan Page

10. 'What if I can't understand their feelings in Step 2?'

You probably wouldn't worry about this in simple complaints where empathy may not seem appropriate. However, it can be important if the complaint seems complex or you are puzzled by some aspect of it.

The answer here is to summarize and then ask, eg, 'How do you feel about this?' The employee will almost certainly tell you. If he says, eg, 'I'm really angry about it', you can respond with, 'Yes, I can see you're upset.'

11. 'What if they've no ideas and I know the answer?'

You have asked for ideas and there are none forthcoming. You are then itching to tell the employee what to do.

If the problem seems to be outside the employee's training and experience then ask, 'How about...?'

There is little point in persevering with coaching questions if the employee has a gap in his knowledge and experience; this may make the employee feel inadequate. When you ask 'How about...?' you help the employee to learn something *and* let him agree gracefully with your idea.

12. 'What if I don't like their ideas but I'm not sure why?'

We've all probably had this experience when we ask, 'What suggestions do you have?' Then we don't like the answer. The chances are that you were vague in stating your position so that you yourself don't know what will fit it. Or the idea could be truly revolutionary. Here are some ideas.

You can ask, 'How would (that idea) fit with (a current policy)?' Or, 'How would that affect the whatsitsname?' If the employee doesn't know, you can suggest that he take some time to think about it.

You can ask why the employee made that suggestion. This gives you some thinking time.

You could say that you need time to think over the employee's suggestion. If you do this, schedule some thinking time in your diary. Otherwise, when you come to the follow-up date you will still be uneasy.

13. 'What if their problem is very personal?'

Even if you don't want to get involved you can still go through Steps 1 and 2 but without delving too deeply (you *fully understand* that it is a personal problem and you can say so).

In Step 3 you could safely say, 'I'd like to help *so far as I can,* but I'm no expert.' In Step 4 you can ask, 'Who else have you talked with?' Then you may ask, 'Have you thought about the CAB (Citizens Advice Bureau – in the UK), your doctor, spouse, etc?' Step 5 may then involve allowing some time off to see an expert.

Pleasant exceptions

Probably the best one is where it rapidly becomes clear that the employee is complaining about the present situation because they have an idea to put forward.

You agree that the situation might be improved (it's a rare one that can't), ask the employee to present his ideas, and he does so in a highly organized way. At the end you ask questions to test his thinking and to satisfy your curiosity, then say, 'That's fine by me. Go ahead, and let me know when you've finished. When will that be?' (Always set a specific follow-up date.)

Another nice exception is where an emotional employee comes to you with a problem he couldn't handle. You patiently listen without comment. You show that you understand his feelings and thank him for raising the matter because you don't want one of your people to have this sort of problem (Step 3).

You say that you would like to see the problem put right and they respond, 'Well I hoped you would but don't worry, I know what to do now. Just talking about it has been a great help. Thank you for listening.'

Notes

TRYING IT OUT

ONE STEP AT A TIME, THEN ALL TOGETHER

People learn by *doing*, by reflecting on how it went, and by working out how to improve. So please plan to use this framework, and *carry out your plan*.

The good news is that you can build up or, more likely, enhance these skills on the job by trying them out one at a time. Then you can combine one or more of them. Further good news is that you don't have to be handling a real complaint in order to practise the skills, just about any work-centred discussion will do.

If you build up your skills from the next few pages you will be able to put all the steps together when a real complaint comes along. To prepare for that event you can rehearse using the whole framework with a colleague or your boss, or a trainer. There is provision for this at the end of this section. You can ask your boss for advice if you wish.

By now you know that the framework is sensible so stick with it; then you will be able to control yourself and the discussion. Trouble comes when you don't move from step to step in a deliberate fashion. If you should find that you have lost your way, check where you are in the framework.

The important thing is to try it out; don't just read about it and hope you will somehow remember in the future. Try it out, learn from the experience and try again.

The chances are that you will get most things mostly right first time round. If you experience any difficulties you probably won't need much help to get over them. The tips that follow are therefore very small ones.

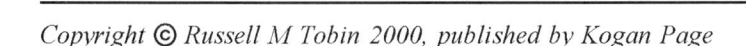

> **1. Listen attentively to the employee's complaint, ensure that you fully understand it, take notes.**

Don't worry for the moment about identifying a complaint, just practise listening. And here, to help you, we repeat a useful definition of good listening.

> 'You should be able to express the speaker's ideas in your own words – to his satisfaction – before you react.'

Not a lot of people are good at listening but it is such a powerful skill that you will notice pleased reactions – and pleasing work results – when you do it well. Look back to pages 59–64 and work at applying the high-scoring tips. Also, if you have the Practical Leadership Skills workbook, look again at Skill No. 4 in there.

Action plan

> At work, note how often you summarize what someone has said. Also check if you ever come in with your own remarks as soon as a speaker stops, so they can't know if you understood or even heard them. Try it at home too.
>
> See how the conversation gets a new impetus each time you summarize or clarify understanding. Check if agreed action is more appropriate after good listening.

Result

> How are you doing; how do you need to improve?

> **2. Show that you understand his feelings and thank him for raising the matter.**

The ability to listen and empathize will win you friends and influence people, but you have to work at it. Think about your social life and how you show that you understand people's feelings, eg, 'That must be a nuisance for you', and so on. You empathize outside work so try, where appropriate, to do the same *at* work.

Action plan

(a) Ask your colleagues how you appear to them; do you seem concerned only about the work, with no concern for people? Or do you seem to appreciate people's feelings (even though you may not agree with them) without losing your objectivity?

(b) As you listen to people speaking about their problems, ask yourself how they must feel, eg, frustrated, upset, powerless, whatever? In your own way *show* that you understand how they feel. If you don't show them, they may think you don't care.

(c) If they are speaking about something that is clearly serious and you can't understand how they feel – ask how they feel. They'll usually be ready to tell you.

(d) Even when you don't like what people are telling you, try to appreciate the courage they have in raising the matter, and thank them for raising it. Then they won't bottle things up.

Result

How are you doing; how do you need to improve?

> **3. State your own position undefensively and without hostility.**

You can state your position in any type of work discussion, not just complaints. Your position may comprise negative *and* positive elements, eg, 'I didn't know but I want to see it fixed.' Or, 'I'd like to help but I have too much work.'

You can work from first principles ('Stealing is wrong, it must stop'). You can provide direction, even if it is not very precise ('That doesn't seem right, we ought to do something about it'). Another way to give yourself room to manoeuvre is to say something like, 'My first reaction is...'

You may disagree with what you hear but find it difficult to formulate a reason. In such cases you can give yourself time to think with, eg, 'I can't go along with that'.

Action plan

> (a) Add your own ideas to the above and, when you want to influence the direction of a discussion, try out your options as appropriate.
>
> (b) Don't try to defend the indefensible. This angers people and they will attack you. To say you're sorry about a situation is not admitting responsibility.
>
> (c) If you don't want to be diverted from your position use the 'cracked record' technique, ie repeat your position using the same or different words.

Result

> How are you doing; how do you need to improve?

Are you finding that people work better with you when they know where you stand?

> **4. Find out if the employee has any suggestions for resolving his complaint.**

This can be hard when you want to jump to Step 5. Or easy when you have no solution yourself and can acknowledge that the employee is closer to the problem than you are.

From the demonstrations you have seen how the employee's position in Steps 1 and 2 combines with your position in Step 3 to give a joint platform for moving forward. It is best if you define the problem after those three steps and then use the employee to devise a solution where possible.

Action plan

> (a) When appropriate try summarizing the discussion so far. At the same time, focus on the problem now to be solved and ask, 'What suggestions do you have?', or 'What options do we have?', etc.
>
> (b) If at first you get no suggestions, try restating the problem in a different way. Or you could try, eg, 'How do you see the problem?'
>
> (c) If you get suggestions which conflict with your position, then restate your position. Use the 'cracked record' technique if you keep getting bad ideas.
>
> (d) If it is obvious that the employee has no ideas, and is not likely to have, then ask, 'How would you feel about (your idea for a solution)?'

Result

> How are you doing; how do you need to improve?

You should find that people are often ready with ideas – if you seek them. You will also find that you prefer listening to their ideas rather than seeking their approval for yours.

Copyright © Russell M Tobin 2000, published by Kogan Page

> **5. If applicable, specify what you will do to correct the situation.**

Please: only, if applicable. Avoid taking on work that the employee could do. Or doing something that is not appropriate. There are several options for this step.

First, agreeing to a suggestion from the employee, eg, 'Could you (the boss) do such and such?'

Second, your own thinking, eg, 'And what I'll do is...'

Third, negative action, where you specify, eg, 'Okay, Fred, it looks like it's all with you then.'

Fourth, vague action, eg, 'Let me think about it'. Avoid this one because, without a specific follow-up date, the problem gets swept under the carpet. But you can leave the employee to think about it just as well and get him to report back to you rather than you reporting back to him.

Action plan

> (a) This is simple. Never, promise to do something that you should not be doing; delegate all you can.
>
> (b) At the end of a discussion always be quite specific about which of you will now do what. Try getting the employee to summarise what he will do.
>
> (c) Where one or both of you have to report back, get the date entered in your diary.

Result

> How are you doing; how do you need to improve?

Are you thinking before you commit yourself? Do you find that this step brings a discussion to a clearly defined end? Do employees seem clearer about what they will do?

REHEARSAL EXERCISE

A rehearsal pulls together the skills you have been trying out separately. However, it may be difficult to rehearse this type of discussion because knowledge of a problem and thus the initiative lies with someone else.

Even so, you can ask yourself if there are any problems simmering that you would like someone to bring into the open? Does someone seem to have a problem but is not raising it with you? Are there any situations which you think may not have been dealt with 100 per cent satisfactorily?

If so, all you need do is approach the person concerned and ask, 'How's it going with the thingy?' Then switch to listening attentively and bingo, you're in Step 1.

The questions overleaf will help you prepare for a discussion. You may also wish to re-read one or more demonstrations before you attempt this exercise. If nothing comes quickly to mind, you can look back to pages 55 to 58 (Comparisons) for some ideas.

You can practise handling a situation by asking a colleague (or boss or trainer) to take the role of an employee – or even of another colleague. Brief him or her with page 127.

After your practice ask the 'employee' for feedback on how you followed the steps in this framework, and the skills in the PLS framework. Ask how he felt about the way you handled him.

If you tape record the practice this helps you appreciate the feedback, and you can reflect on how your behaviour would have influenced *you* if you had been in the 'employee' seat.

It may be useful to repeat the practice, trying different ways of following the steps, and with the 'employee' being more difficult, or raising different problems. You should still follow the framework (just concentrate more) so that you are controlling your own behaviour rather than reacting to his.

Don't be afraid of having available the small card at the end of the book.

NB   The next two pages are the only ones that you may photocopy. You can thus rehearse as many discussions as you like over time.

Handling Employees' Problems

Your own viewpoint (as boss)

This helps you decide if you should try to have the discussion at all. Please note that the clarification process below is not the same as the notes shown on page 128.

a. *What knowledge do you have about the matter complained of – BEFORE receiving the complaint? Distinguish between facts and assumptions, between rumours and first-hand information. (If you want to handle a complaint about which you have no prior knowledge leave this page blank, the 'employee' will be able to think of something. That's okay, in fact, it's a better test of your skills – and the framework.)*

b. *How might the 'employee' feel about the situation? What would be the final straw that brings him to you instead of handling the problem himself? (You might find you get this wrong, but hazard a guess.)*

c. *What is your likely position regarding the matter complained of? Note positive and negative aspects, company policy if applicable, etc. (You may wish to talk with your own boss about this if you would like guidance.) You should be prepared to adjust your position according to the real information you receive from the 'employee'.*

d. *Given (a), (b), and (c) above, how do you think the* **total** *problem might be defined, ie the problem which now has to be solved? (But don't get locked into this or you won't listen to the 'employee' who may say something quite unexpected.)*

e. *In coaching the 'employee' to come up with a solution, are there any areas of his training or experience that you should ask the 'employee' to consider?*

f. *What actions to correct the situation are properly for you – and only you – to take? (Again, don't get locked in to these ideas; the discussion may turn out quite differently.)*

Copyright © Russell M Tobin 2000, published by Kogan Page

The employee's viewpoint

Use this page to brief the stand-in 'employee' with whom you will practise.

g. What is the 'employee' complaining about – as HE sees it? (If you want to handle a complaint about which you have no prior knowledge, that is okay, leave this page for the 'employee' to complete – it could be about almost anything.)

h. What is the 'employee' likely to feel most strongly about, eg, the problem itself, the way he is affected, the other people involved, etc.?

i. If you ask for ideas for solving the problem, what ideas might the 'employee' have? (But don't expect the 'employee' necessarily to raise these ideas; he may have his own.)

For the stand-in 'employee'

j. The aim of this exercise is for the 'boss' to practise using a framework of critical steps to handle a complaint from an employee or colleague. You should react according to the way you are handled. The information above is what the 'boss' thinks the real-life 'employee' *may* say. *You* may come up with something different to the above, depending on how well you relate to the situation and how well you know the real-life employee.

k. After the practice please try to give objective feedback about how the 'boss' followed each step of the framework, and how you felt regarding the way you were handled. Especially how the boss listened and understood all you said.

Thank you for helping the 'boss' to enhance his skills.

Taking notes during the discussion

> When you follow-up on a plan, it is useful to have the notes made during the discussion. During the first demonstration (on a cash-flow problem, page 14) the boss made notes which are shown below.
>
> As he was unable to prepare for the discussion, the boss noted only the step numbers and ticked off each part of each step, or made notes, as he went through the framework.
>
> NB You will notice that the notes are only what is needed to jog the boss's memory. You may note more or less.

1. *Savings*   £100 p.m.   ✓

2. ✓   ✓

3. *Personal*   ✓

4. *Options* → *HP*

5. ———

F/U   19/9

SUMMARY

This workbook has taken you through a framework of critical steps for handling problems that employees bring to you. It has shown how these discussions can be used to develop employees through coaching and delegation.

It is hard to foresee what problems employees may raise. What you can foresee is the need for some sort of structure for handling them, the framework discussed here. It needs to be used in a deliberate manner but it still allows flexibility.

HANDLING EMPLOYEES' PROBLEMS

1. Listen attentively to the employee's complaint, ensure that you fully understand it, take notes.

2. Show that you understand his feelings and thank him for raising the matter.

3. State your own position undefensively and without hostility.

4. Find out if the employee has any suggestions for resolving his complaint.

5. If applicable, specify what you will do to correct the situation.

You have seen the value of active listening, and of empathy. These can be hard skills to master so you may have to work at them – constantly. But communication is a major part of your job – and listening is half of communication.

Stating your own position, firmly or even only tentatively, helps to create a joint platform for problem-solving.

You will have noticed in the demonstrations that the framework can be used with two or more people, and that the proportion of time used for each step varies according to the situation. The same will apply back at your workplace.

This framework, together with Practical Leadership Skills, helps you to control your own behaviour and thus influence the behaviour of others. It helps to generate solutions to problems through good teamwork. And, as you reduce your own workload, you make more time for coaching.

Copyright © Russell M Tobin 2000, published by Kogan Page

WORKING TOWARDS A QUALIFICATION?

This workbook, and others in the series, will help you gain the NVQ unit in 'Managing People'. Because the workbook deals only with interpersonal skills, and specifically with handling problems that people bring to you, it will not match all the elements in that unit.

However, this coaching style of interpersonal skills can only be used effectively if supported by your knowledge of organisation values, policies, and procedures; of the products and services you supply, your standards of service, levels of authority, etc.

Assessment

For the assessor to decide if you meet the criteria for the NVQ unit on 'Managing People' you may be asked:

- questions on all the topics in the unit;

- to simulate interactions with employees, eg handling a complaint, a grievance or a work problem.

Other modules in this series will help with further types of interactions.

Good luck!

A REMINDER CARD

If you would like to have a reminder to keep in your pocket, or desk drawer, or personal organizer, you can cut out the card below.

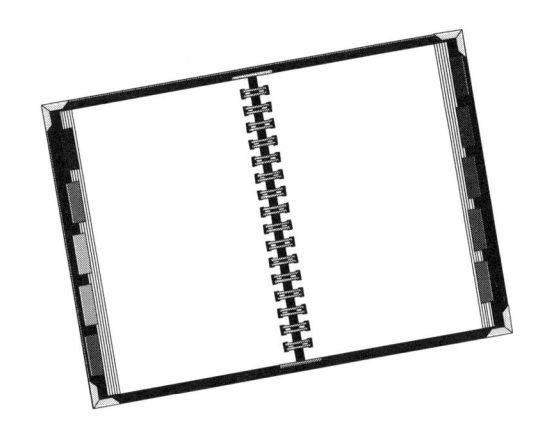

HANDLING EMPLOYEES' PROBLEMS	**PRACTICAL LEADERSHIP SKILLS**
1. Listen attentively to the employee's complaint, ensure that you fully understand it, take notes.	1. Maintain or enhance the self-esteem of the employee.
2. Show that you understand his feelings and thank him for raising the matter.	2. Don't attack the person, FOCUS ON THE PROBLEM.
3. State your own position undefensively and without hostility.	3. Don't assume that the employee has committed an offence.
4. Find out if the employee has any suggestions for resolving his complaint.	4. Encourage the employee to express his opinions and make suggestions.
5. If applicable, specify what you will do to correct the situation.	5. Allow the employee adequate time to think through the problem and to suggest a solution.
Copyright © Russell M Tobin 2000	6. Ensure that the employee has an appropriate ACTION programme.
	7. Always set a specific follow-up date.

Visit Kogan Page on-line

Comprehensive information on Kogan Page titles

Features include

- complete catalogue listings, including book reviews and descriptions

- special monthly promotions

- information on NEW titles and BESTSELLING titles

- a secure shopping basket facility for on-line ordering

PLUS everything you need to know about KOGAN PAGE

http://www.kogan-page.co.uk